*I'd Like to
Call for Help,
but
I Don't Know
the Number*

I'd Like to Call for Help, but I Don't Know the Number

THE SEARCH FOR SPIRITUALITY IN EVERYDAY LIFE

Abraham J. Twerski, M.D.

3669

PHAROS BOOKS
A SCRIPPS HOWARD COMPANY
NEW YORK

First published in 1991.

Library of Congress Cataloging-in-Publication Data
Twerski, Abraham J.
I'd like to call for help, but I don't know the number:
the search for the spirituality in everyday life / Abraham J. Twerski.
p.   cm.
ISBN 0-88687-648-6 : $14.95
1. Spiritual life. 2. Twelve-step programs.   I. Title.
BL624.5.T84   1991
291.4—dc20   91-18629   CIP

Printed in the United States of America

Design by Janet Tingey

Pharos Books
A Scripps Howard Company
200 Park Avenue
New York, NY 10166

10 9 8 7 6 5 4 3 2 1

Pharos Books are available at special discounts on bulk
purchases for sales promotions, premiums, fundraising or
educational use. For details, contact
the Special Sales Department, Pharos Books,
200 Park Avenue, New York, NY 10166

*Friends, staff and clients of
Gateway Rehabilitation Center
past, present and future*

CONTENTS

Spirituality in Recovery

The way the concept of spirituality is approached in this book requires some explanation, and it might be best explained by relating how I came to deal with it.

My first occupation was as a cleric. I had grown up under the tutelage of my father who was a rabbi *extraordinaire*, and I had hoped to follow in his footsteps, to provide counseling for the bewildered and comfort for the suffering. However, I entered my calling in the post-World War II era, when psychiatry and psychology were in their apogee, and when man, intoxicated with the grandiosity of his epochal scientific advances—antibiotics and other wonder drugs on the one hand and nuclear energy on the other—entered into the "God is dead" era. These unprecedented productions of the human genius gave rise to an attitude that man himself is indeed omnipotent, and there was therefore no room for two omnipotent beings. Psychiatry and psychology, having the imprimatur of science, became the basis of human conduct and the key to the attainment of happiness.

It appeared to me that my function as a rabbi would not be at all like that of my father. Rather, I would be relegated to conducting services, performing marriage and burial rituals, and preaching. In short, to be a functionary. This was not what I had envisioned for myself. If I wished to be a counselor or a comforter, I would have to utilize the authoritative methods of science, and this called for training in medicine and psychology to become a psychiatrist.

Four years of medical school at Milwaukee's Marquette University and a year of internship at that city's Mount Sinai Hospital qualified me to practice medicine, and three years of post-graduate psychiatric training at the University of Pittsburgh's Western Psychiatric Institute provided me with the basis for diagnosing and treating emotional and mental disorders.

While psychiatric training brought me in direct contact with much human suffering and with various complex theories on the formation of thought and emotion, midway in psychiatric training I began treating a woman who profoundly affected my career.

I had been assigned one day to duty in the "walk-in-clinic," where patients with an urgent need to consult a psychiatrist could be seen without a previous appointment. One of the clients that day was Isabelle, a woman in her sixties, whose case helped fashion my professional career. Isabelle had developed a dependency on alcohol early in life and, being the daughter of an Episcopalian priest, she alienated the family by her unacceptable conduct. Her husband became intolerant of her drinking and made it clear that the marriage could not continue unless the alcohol was eliminated. "I knew that I could not stop drinking," Isabelle said, "and that I was not being a good wife or mother." She complied with her husband's request for a divorce, and never saw him or her child again.

Being a very attractive woman, her companionship was widely sought, and her escorts provided her with an abundance of alcohol. As the drinking began to take its inevitable toll, she began a gradual descent on the social ladder, eventually culminating in a skid-row existence. For some twenty years she was in and out of hospitals for drying-out after alcoholic binges, and in the process made the perfunctory visits to Alcoholics Anonymous meetings that were required by the people who ran the hospital "drunk-tank."

At age 56, Isabelle did a rather strange thing. She contacted an attorney friend and insisted that he have her committed to the state mental hospital for one year as an inebriate. Upon completion of this year of enforced abstinence, Isabelle found herself a job as a housekeeper, and became an active participant in Alcoholics Anonymous. When she came for her psychiatric consultation, she was in her fifth year of sobriety.

I cannot recall the initial reason Isabelle gave for requesting psychiatric treatment. Whatever it was obviously did not impress me. I was fascinated, however, by her decision to place herself in a mental hospital for a full year in order to enable her life to take a new direction. As a fledgling psychiatrist, I was deeply interested in human motivation, and I was puzzled by what could have motivated this woman to take so drastic a step. What was there to be gained by being sober? Certainly not reconciliation with her family, because they had written her off as dead, and did not acknowledge any of her overtures, even after she had been sober for several years. Curious to discover the source of her motivation, I encouraged Isabelle to continue in psychotherapy, and so began a relationship of thirteen years duration.

Isabelle frequently referred to her participation in Alcoholics

Anonymous, of which I knew next to nothing. This further aroused my curiosity. In medical school, treatment of alcoholism had not even received mention because it was assumed there was no treatment. The medical student's contact with an alcoholic occurred when some medical crisis consequent to drinking compelled the emergency room staff to admit the individual. The doctor's role was to pull the patient through the crisis and send him out to the inevitable return to drinking. Since no courses on alcoholism were included in the psychiatric curriculum either, it was evident to me that psychiatry had nothing to offer these incorrigible drinkers. Yet, here was a group of people who had somehow found a method of achieving what the best minds in psychiatry could not achieve. In an effort to discover the therapeutic secrets of AA I began to attend their meetings.

Had I not been a cleric earlier, I would probably not have been as deeply impressed with AA. However, two features of this program had a profound impact upon me.

Whereas all people are equal in the eyes of God, this lofty concept cannot always be implemented in institutionalized religion. Most religious denominations have buildings, places of worship. A building costs money, as does its operation and maintenance. A church or synagogue requires a staff, whose livelihood must be provided. In short, any religious institution has a budget which it must meet, and invariably this is achieved by contributions from the membership.

This creates a problem. A very affluent member may contribute a major portion of the budget, while someone of modest means may be able to make only a small contribution. While rich and poor are equal in the eyes of God, the cleric may be faced with the reality that he cannot risk offending an affluent member upon whose contribution he must so heavily rely. Sometimes even the most idealistic cleric may not be able to avoid this favoritism, which is, at least in theory, incompatible with the principles of religion.

It was therefore a novel and refreshing experience to discover the egalitarianism in AA. In the meeting rooms, all are equal. The money and prestige of the affluent can buy them nothing in AA. I recall one AA meeting where two women, Nancy and Edith, were engaged in a discussion, sitting side by side, each holding a cup of coffee and a doughnut. Nancy had come to the meeting in her luxury automobile, while Edith had to have the group secretary sign a slip for her so that she might recover the bus fare from the welfare agency, because otherwise she could not afford to come to meetings. Nancy's wealth could not buy her any special privileges in AA, because there were none to be had. In that meeting room these two strikingly different individuals were two suffering human beings trying to restore a degree of sanity to their lives.

I was also impressed by the dedication of people in AA to help one another. This is not to say that many acts of kindness do not occur elsewhere. Of course they do. But I wonder what response I might have received had I awakened one of the members of my congregation on a frigid winter night and asked him to please go to the home of a fellow parishioner who is emotionally distraught. I suspect that the person I awakened from a sound sleep would have questioned *my* sanity. "Rabbi," he would have said, "are you aware that it is 2:00 a.m.? If Sam is so emotionally upset, why doesn't he see a doctor? What am I supposed to do for him in the middle of the night, and why are you calling *me*?"

However, when a recovering alcoholic is awakened on a frigid night because some drunk thinks he wants help, he will pull himself out of bed and make his way along icy roads to the caller's home, knowing full well that by the time he arrives the person may have had a marked change of heart, and his belligerence and hostility toward anyone who attempts to preach abstinence to him may resolve in the helper being thrown down the stairs. Or perhaps, even if he is welcomed, the slobbering drunk may embrace him and proceed to throw up all over him. All this notwithstanding, the person who is experiencing recovery reaches out to help another sufferer. I do not mean to be harsh with religion, because it has so much to offer. Yet I cannot deny that some of the principles of religion may find greater expression in AA.

When I assumed the position as Director of Psychiatry at Pittsburgh's St. Francis Hospital, I inherited a huge alcohol detoxification unit and outpatient clinic. Several years later, I founded Gateway, a large rehabilitation center for treatment of alcoholism and drug addiction. I have thus been totally immersed in the treatment of these conditions.

Great emphasis is placed on the pivotal role of spirituality in recovery from alcoholism and drug addiction. For all its importance, spirituality remains a rather vague concept, and means different things to different people. The purpose of this book is to shed some additional light on this vital concept in recovery.

Many people assume spirituality to be synonymous with religion. Some people who are uncomfortable with religion may therefore have some difficulty with spirituality. This is further compounded by the reference in AA to a Higher Power—God, as I understand Him—which implies that recovery from alcoholism or drug addiction, at least via the twelve-step route, is contingent upon belief in God. People who profess to be atheists may thus be reluctant to embrace a program which emphasizes spirituality. It is my hope to demonstrate that spirituality need not be dependent on religion. It is of interest that this emphasis on spirituality is not widely encountered in treatment of emotional disorders other than the addictions. If, as I hope to demonstrate, spirituality, whether of a religious character or otherwise, is indeed a necessary component of emotional health, this omission is to be deplored.

Ironically, the alcoholic or drug addict may actually be fortunate in that his condition results in a crisis that forces him to confront the role or absence of spirituality in his life. Lacking such a crisis, many people may live their entire lives without coming to a fulfillment of the spiritual component in their lives, and hence never realize their full potential.

I believe that there are few if any differences in the emotional needs of the alcoholic versus the nonalcoholic. It is only that in the alcoholic or addict these needs are much more prominent and better defined, and hence can more easily be addressed.

Several years ago I was asked to provide material on spirituality derived from Jewish theological writings for the recovering Jewish alcoholic or addict. To my surprise, this book, *Living Each Day* (Mesorah Publications), has found wide popularity among people who never had any problem with addiction, thus confirming for me that concepts about spirituality that were specifically intended to meet the needs of the addicted individual have equal relevance to the nonaddict.

Lest anyone have any doubts, let me point out that in my role as a physician, I do not have any interest in promoting religion. My goal is to help people overcome their emotional problems in a manner that produces mental health. I leave the task of expounding on religion in the able hands of the clergy. I do not wish to convert anyone to any specific religion or to religion as a whole.

Although I may quote the scriptures and other theological writings in elaborating on spirituality, this need not imply that spirituality can be achieved only through religion. While there are specific religious references to spirituality, I invite the nonreligious reader to consider them at their face value, and if they are incompatible with his belief or nonbelief, to feel free to reject them. I trust that enough substance will remain even after this winnowing process to be of value to even an ardent atheist.

So let us begin together to investigate the rather elusive but all-important concept of spirituality.

CHAPTER 1

Is Man Homo Sapiens?

Being human is difficult. Becoming human is a life long
process. To be truly human is a gift.
ABRAHAM HESCHE

The noted historian, Barbara Tuchman, wrote in the *Saturday
Review* in December 1966, "Let us beware of the plight of our
colleagues, the behavioral scientists, who by use of a proliferat-
ing jargon have painted themselves into a corner—or isolation
ward—of unintelligibility. *They* know what they mean, but no
one else does. Psychologists and sociologists are farthest gone
in the disease and probably incurable. Their condition might be
pitied if one did not suspect it was deliberate. Their retreat into
the arcane is meant to set them apart from the great unlearned,
to mark their possession of some unshared, unsharable expertise."

Discussions of things such as spirituality often feature long
words and difficult-to-grasp arguments. In contrast to those
behavioral scientists described by Ms. Tuchman, I do not
possess any unshared or unsharable expertise, and I hope to
avoid the pitfall of unintelligibility. I have been impressed by

the effectiveness of the AA teaching to "keep it simple," and in compliance with this principle, I wish to make a simple assertion: *Man is different from animals*.

This hardly seems a shocking revelation, even after we eliminate the obvious difference that man is a biped with an upright posture. Yet a bit of reflection shows us that the true distinctions between man and animal are not universally acknowledged. For example, biologists have classified man as being *homo sapiens, homo* referring to the general group of hominoids, among which are monkeys, apes, orangutans, and chimpanzees, and *sapiens* (intellect) being the distinctive feature that separates man from other animals.

Perhaps it is my ego at work that makes me reject this classification, according to which I am an "intellectual gorilla." Indeed, I believe that other forms of life also have intellect, but are not as wise as man. Hence, the biologic appellation distinguishes man from animal only quantitatively; i.e., we have *more* intellect than animals, but does not provide a *qualitative* distinction.

I believe that more than just a greater degree of intelligence distinguishes man from animals, and that if we analyze man and understand all that we can about him—his thoughts, emotions, behavior—we will find additional features that are uniquely human. On this basis, I would like to coin a definition. All the unique features of a human being *in their totality* are what constitute the *spirit* of man. When man exercises these unique features, he is being *spiritual*. Thus, *spirituality* is simply the implementation of those distinctive features that separate man from animal.

I realize that I am treading on thin ice, because I may be challenged to prove that all these features are indeed unique to man. You might say, "How do you know that animals do not have the equivalent of Beethoven's Ninth Symphony or

Shakespeare's *Hamlet*? Just as animals may well be unaware that these exist among humans, humans may be ignorant of what exists among animals."

Absolutely correct. Yet no one has really taken issue with the biologic establishment for designating man as *homo sapiens*, and no one argues that animals may indeed be far more intelligent than we assume, and that we are merely ignorant of the great intellectual achievements of animals. Someone might argue that bees are extraordinary mathematicians and engineers, who have not only calculated the configuration of a hexagon to an unbelievable degree of precision, but have also cleverly devised a structural technique that they have communicated to their brethren all over the world. While this might conceivably be true, we generally do not assume this to be so. Rather, we attribute the geometrically precise honeycomb to an inborn instinct rather than to bees' mathematical genius.

I believe we are justified in extending this way of thinking to other properties that we consider lacking in animals. We generally assume that animals do not create poetry or produce artistic masterpieces, and that animals have not transmitted the history of ancient events to their offspring over many generations. While this is indeed only an assumption, it is a reasonable one, and one that an overwhelming number of people hold to be valid. I will therefore proceed on the basis of this assumption that, given our observation of animals, man displays sensitivities and attributes of a unique nature. It is in the quality of these unique attributes that his spirituality lies.

CHAPTER 2

Spirituality and Free Choice

The last of the human freedoms is to choose one's attitudes.

VICTOR FRANKL

One of the ways in which man is distinct from animal is that man is free, whereas animals are not.

Man and animals both have biologic drives: hunger, thirst, sex, desire for comfort, avoidance of pain, etc. Animals are at the mercy of their biologic drives and cannot resist them. An animal that is hungry is driven to look for food, one that is thirsty must look for water, and one that is in heat must look for a mate. Given our right to reach certain conclusions, as was discussed in the previous chapter, we may assume that no animal has ever made a conscious decision, "I will suffer the pangs of hunger and thirst, but I will not eat or drink today, because I have decided to fast." Nor has it ever happened that an animal in heat has suppressed its sexual urge and made a conscious choice of celibacy. Animals do not have the capacity to choose in this sense. They are totally dominated by their internal impulses, and lack freedom of choice.

True, under certain circumstances an animal may avoid gratifying a biologic drive. For example, a hungry jackal looking for food may come across a delectable carcass, but if this happens to be in the possession of a ferocious tiger, he will not approach it. However, this is not because he consciously suppresses his appetite, but because the fear of being killed by the tiger overrides the hunger. This is not an instance of free choice, but merely a greater biologic drive, that of survival, overcoming a lesser drive, that of hunger.

Some psychologists would have us believe that human behavior is on the same plane, and that man's freedom of will is but an illusion. They argue that man has a number of drives, some of which are in conflict with others, and that human behavior is merely the result of the struggle among various drives for dominance. They claim that man's consciousness of what he is doing causes him to *think* that he is choosing, but that this is nothing more than an illusion. His choices are being made for him by his internal drives.

These psychologists may be in concert with those biologists who consider man as merely another variety of animal, and according to this concept it is virtually meaningless to speak of spirituality. It is quite evident, however, that in practice we do not subscribe to this theory. Our entire concept of human responsibility, with our elaborate system of positive and negative sanctions, is based on the assumption that man is not at the mercy of his impulses, and that he indeed has the freedom to choose and determine much of his behavior.

Freedom is one of man's preeminent values. Patrick Henry spoke for all humanity when he said, "Give me liberty or give me death," as did the founding fathers when they asserted that man has an inalienable right to life, liberty, and the pursuit of happiness. Tyranny is intolerable, and is equally despicable when it is that of internal drives as when it is that of a ruthless despot. Slavery is abhorrent, not only because it is often cruel, but more so because it is dehumanizing. Man is a free creature, and to take away his freedom is to rob him of his humanity.

Man is free when he has the capacity to make a free choice. In contrast to animals, man need not be dominated by his biologic drives. However, if a person avoids gratifying a given biologic drive only out of fear of consequences, he is still not behaving on a true human level, because as we have seen, animals are also deterred by fear of punishment. Whether the punishment is death or corporeal pain or imprisonment or social condemnation is immaterial. The person who avoids stealing because of the fear of being apprehended and punished, or who avoids an illicit sexual relation because of the fear of contracting disease or being condemned by society or family is really no different than the hungry jackal who avoids the carcass that is in the possession of a tiger.

Man functions in his unique human capacity when he chooses to deny an urge even when there is no possibility of any unpleasant consequences. When his decision to deny his biologic drive is based only on his principles of right and wrong, man rises to a supra-animal level. This is when man makes a free moral choice, something which is uniquely human, and which is beyond the capabilities of even the most intelligent animal.

A person may be an intellectual genius, capable of the most sophisticated abstract thinking. He may be the world's greatest scientist and be the ultimate in *sapiens*, but if he is incapable of making a free moral choice, he is lacking a fundamental feature of humanness.

The importance of making a free moral choice is nowhere as evident as in addiction. Whereas there have been various types of slavery in world history, none has been as total and as absolute as the slavery of addiction. Whatever form the addiction may take, whether alcohol, drugs, sex, food, or gambling, it totally dominates the individual. Everything in life becomes subordinate to complying with the demands of the addiction. I have heard this from many recovering people, one of whom said, "It has been twenty-one years since I drank. I may drink today, but if I do it will be because I choose to do so. I am no longer compelled. When I was in my addiction, I had no choice."

Achieving self-esteem is crucial in maintaining sobriety, as I have pointed out in *Self-Discovery in Recovery* (Hazelden, 1984). A lack of self-esteem can be found to have been present in most addicts *prior* to the actual onset of the addiction. As the addiction progresses and deprives the person of the capacity to make a free moral choice in regard to his addiction, his self-concept is further depressed, since the person feels himself to be lacking in the very capacity that defines his humanity.

The human uniqueness of the capacity to make a free moral choice is a major component of the spirit, and exercising this capacity is being spiritual. It is clear that even a person who does not have a religious orientation can conceptualize himself as being free, and is thus capable of being spiritual.

CHAPTER 3

Contentment

The purpose of man's life is not happiness but worthiness.
FELIX ADLER

Closely related to gratification of biologic drives is the pursuit of contentment. Indeed, since contentment is essentially being free of distress, it too is the goal of a biologic drive, because all living things seek to avoid discomfort of any type. The human being is no exception, and we can hardly fault a person for wishing to be content.

It is clear, however, that people often voluntarily accept some discontent. When the alarm rings in the morning, one would really prefer to turn it off and get back to pleasant slumber. When one drags himself out of bed to get on with the work day, one is actually frustrating a natural desire, and this is only because of a goal that supersedes the desire for physical contentment. The goal of earning one's livelihood and supporting one's family overrides the natural tendency to continue sleeping. This is a prototype of accepting a degree of discomfort or making a sacrifice for the sake of an ultimate goal.

This concept is of great importance in the prevention of addiction. When the rather naive campaign was launched, urging youngsters to "Just say no to drugs," some adolescents who were interviewed responded, "Why?" What else is there?"

There is no denying that alcohol and other mind-altering substances give the user some type of pleasant sensation. Even if the "high" does not constitute a state of euphoria, it is at least a respite from unpleasant sensations of anxiety, tension, and depression, and awkward self-consciousness. The use of such chemicals is nothing other than the pursuit of contentment.

But why should young people risk the serious social, physical, and psychological consequences of mind-altering chemicals? Are there no other, safer, and more durable ways of achieving a feeling of contentment?

Of course there are. The problem is that (1) these do not yield immediate results, and (2) one must have sufficient self-confidence that one's efforts can ultimately achieve the desired state of contentment.

The problem of immediacy is relatively new in the history of mankind, and may explain why the use of mind-altering substances is much more prevalent now than in previous times.

Years ago people were accustomed to waiting. Travel by covered wagon was of weeks duration, as was mail by pony express. Foods would cook slowly over a period of hours, and transactions involving long columns of figures had to be laboriously calculated and rechecked. The miracles of technology have virtually eliminated all waiting. Jet flight, the telephone, and fax machines have made communications seem instantaneous. Precooked food and microwaves have eliminated time-delay in food preparation, and the magic of computers has reduced complex mathematical calculations to a fraction of a second. Speed is the password of modern technology, and with the exception of pregnancy, everything appears hurried and produces results that are immediate.

In an ethos where virtually everything is expected to occur instantaneously, it is difficult to impress young people that they should wait for years to achieve a state of well-being. Their quest for a chemical that will provide instant gratification is quite in keeping with everything else that goes on around them.

Even if delay were to be tolerated, this can only be when there is light at the end of the tunnel; i.e., when one feels with reasonable certainty that the desired state of contentment can ultimately be achieved. This requires a degree of self-confidence and an awareness of and trust in one's own capabilities that is so often lacking. In *Like Yourself and Others Will, Too*, (Prentice-Hall, 1978), I pointed out that many people have a distorted self-concept that causes them to be oblivious to their own personality strengths and assets. The nature and complexity of the modern super-industrialized society may have contributed to the prevalence of a negative self-concept. Where there is lack of self-esteem, the aspiration that a state of contentment is achievable is greatly diminished, and with nothing else to look forward to, young people who feel this way are easily attracted to mind-altering chemicals.

High-speed technology will certainly continue its progress, and the wondrous marvels of instant results will continue to erode our tolerance of delay. The solution to the problem of widespread lack of self-esteem remains elusive. Given these facts, what, if anything, can halt the apparent relentless recourse to use of mind-altering chemicals, especially among young people? The only answer is the development of a goal or goals above and beyond that of contentment, something for which people will be willing to forego physical comfort and accept sacrifice, just as one does when one allows the alarm clock to interrupt the nirvana of sleep.

Pride in one's humanness can provide this ultimate goal, but only if one conceptualizes himself as more than *homo sapiens.* The *sapiens* of man is that which brought about air-conditioning, jet flight, the microwave, compact discs, color television, and the many devices and methods whereby man can achieve greater comfort in life. Animals, too, are driven to seek contentment. One producer of dairy products advertises that its raw material is "milk from contented cows." The reasoning underlying this marketing technique is that the highest quality milk is produced by the highest quality cow, and the epitome of excellence in a cow is contentment. Certainly the pride of man should demand a kind of excellence that surpasses that of cows.

The milk producer is unquestionably correct. Contentment is indeed bovine excellence, because cows are creatures without a *spirit.* Spiritual man must be different.

There are an abundance of goals available to man. One person may be interested in the preservation of the environment or in the protection of endangered species. Another may be motivated to combat poverty or improve the lot of the homeless. Yet another may dedicate his efforts to relieve the hunger in famine-stricken countries, and yet another may seek the heights of religious experience and devote himself to fulfillment of religious teachings. There is no dearth of goals available to man, all of which are beyond the capacity of animals, and their uniqueness in the human being makes them components of the human spirit.

The spiritual person is thus one who is willing to sacrifice his personal comfort and physical contentment for a goal external to himself. Development of such spirituality among young people may be the only way in which they may be deterred from the destructive use of mind-altering chemicals. Without such spirituality, neither prohibition, interdiction of drugs at the border, legalization of drugs, nor any other method of enforcement is likely to succeed. Furthermore, absence of chemicals does not lead to elimination of addiction, because lack of spirituality and pursuit of contentment as the ultimate goal will lead to some other type of indulgent behavior. Spirituality in its broadest sense remains mankind's only salvation.

CHAPTER 4

Self-Reflection and Self-Esteem

Everyone is a bore to someone. That is unimportant.
The thing to avoid is being a bore to oneself.
GERALD BRENAN

Do giraffes think about themselves? Does an alligator ever reflect, "I wonder whether I am as good an alligator as I can be?" Do birds or beetles or even chimpanzees make a conscious effort (excluding instinct) to improve or perfect themselves?

These are questions we cannot answer with absolute certainty, because we are not privy to the internal proceedings in the minds of animals. All our conclusions are based on our observation of animals' behavior. It is only an assumption, therefore, but one widely held, that animals do not consciously reflect on themselves. I believe we are justified in proceeding on the premise that conscious reflection on one's self and conscious effort to perfect oneself is unique to man, and as such, it is a component of the *spirit*. When a person consciously reflects on himself, he is being *spiritual*, and when he makes a conscious effort to improve himself, he is being *spiritual*.

One of the obstacles in the path toward spirituality is the reluctance among many people to consciously reflect on themselves. The reason for this became apparent to me as a result of a fortuitous experience.

I have been one of the many victims of chronic low-back pain, and my familiarity with the high risk of addiction when potent painkillers are used for chronic conditions precluded my obtaining any relief from that source. Friends told me of miraculous cures that some people have experienced at mineral spas, but I had dismissed these as old wives' tales. When my position as Director of Psychiatry at an unusually busy mental hospital brought me to a point of burnout, where "getting away from it all" became mandatory, I saw no reason not to avail myself of the total peace and quiet of a mineral spa. Certainly the mineral waters could do no harm.

On the first day at the spa, I was placed in a whirlpool bath in a small cubicle. The experience was nothing less than paradise. I relaxed in the warm water, whose swirling streams gently massaged my entire body. I was at peace, and there was nothing to disturb that peace. After about five or six very enjoyable minutes, I emerged from the bath, telling the attendant how relaxing the experience had been. To my astonishment he said, "You can't get out yet, Sir. The treatment here requires that you stay in the whirlpool for twenty-five minutes."

I returned to the tub, but not to an enjoyable experience. Every minute was an eternity, and after five minutes the situation was no longer tolerable. On my second exodus, the attendant informed me that unless I completed the requisite twenty-five minutes, I could not continue to the next phase of treatment. Not wishing to have spent my money in vain, I returned for fifteen minutes of absolute torture.

Later I reflected on what had been a rude awakening. I had been certain that my distress had been due to the relentless pressures to which I was subject: a busy emergency room, receiving cases around the clock; a 300-bed acute psychiatric hospital for whose coordination and clinical administration I was responsible; serving as back-up for all of the 300 patients if their personal psychiatrist was unavailable; frequent calls from distraught family members, police, lawyers, state government officials, and sundry social agencies. Now I had been temporarily liberated from these overwhelming pressures. Yet I found more than five minutes of peace intolerable! Why?

After a bit of analysis, the answer was apparent. We are all quite adept at diversion, at amusing ourselves one way or another, but many of us are unable to truly relax. We entertain ourselves by reading, watching television, playing golf or cards, chatting with someone, listening to the radio or stereo, or in any of many other ways. But to be entertained is to be *diverted*, for that is what all these activities are: diversions. By focusing our attention on these activities, we divert our attention from other things, from *everything, including ourselves*. When all diversions are eliminated, we are left alone with ourselves, in direct contact with our human condition or conditions that trouble us, and this is where the difficulty lies.

I realized that when left alone in the cubicle in the spa there was no one to talk to, nothing to listen to, nothing to read, nothing to watch, nothing to do. I had been left totally alone, in absolute communion with *myself*! It is a common experience that when one is left alone in a room with someone one dislikes, it can be a very unpleasant experience, and one can hardly wait to get away.

This realization raised the question: what was there about myself that I did not like? Why could I not tolerate being in my own presence? Or was I perhaps completely mistaken in my explanation of the discomfort I experienced in the whirlpool bath?

I hypothesized that I must have some character traits that I would prefer to disown, but whose existence I could ignore only as long as I was distracted by various external preoccupations and stimuli. As I persisted in introspection, I found myself to be a jealous person, often resenting why others had more than I did. I was often vain, trying to impress people. I became aware that when someone offended me, I could hate with a passion. I had temptations and impulses that I thought should be alien to a truly moral person. Why, if people ever discovered what emotions existed beneath the facade that I presented to the world, they would probably reject me. And how could I ever expect to merit Divine blessings if I were indeed a base person?

Along this rather depressing course of introspection, I came across a passage in the Talmud that enabled me to gain a different perspective (Tractate Shabbar 89a). The Talmud explains that the various biblical commandments of behavior were given to man precisely because he has a fundamentally animal body, subject to all the instincts and drives characteristic of subhuman species. Man's distinction is, as we have noted, that he can become master over these impulses. In other words, the discovery of animalistic traits within myself was no reason for me to consider myself to be a "bad" person.

A bit of investigation with my patients confirmed my hypothesis: Many people are indeed incapable of tolerating themselves, because they harbor self-directed feelings of negativity. Their discomfort with themselves may be so great that they employ a variety of tactics, some of them quite drastic, to escape or to deny their identity as they perceive it.

I believe that this sorry state of affairs is the result of a distortion of the self-concept. In other words, these people are in actuality fine, competent, and likeable people. The problem is that they are unaware of this reality. Instead of seeing themselves as they really are, they somehow develop a distorted image of themselves, and it is this distorted image, *which they assume to be the real image*, that becomes intolerable. This hypothesis was further developed in *Like Yourself and Others Will, Too* (Prentice-Hall, 1978), wherein I described a number of behavior patterns and clinical syndromes that are the result of this distorted self-perception. Needless to say, alcoholism and other drug addictions are frequently the result of a person's trying to blot out a self-consciousness that is uncomfortable and which is based on spurious notions of self.

Spirituality relates to what is unique to humans within the animal kingdom and thus requires a valid and accurate self-awareness. As we have seen, this self-awareness may be distorted by negative delusions about one's self. For spirituality to be pervasive, aspects of one's humanity must be viewed realistically.

CHAPTER 5

Growth

Be not afraid of growing slowly, be afraid only of standing still.

CHINESE PROVERB

Animals come into the world according to genetic programming. Their growth is in size and mass only, and when they reach their maximum, the growth stops. Even animals that undergo a physical transformation, such as the tadpole to a frog or the caterpillar to a butterfly do not do so of their own free will. No tadpole has ever succeeded in voluntarily arresting his configuration at the tadpole stage because he did not like the appearance of a frog. Whatever changes occur in animals are programmed in their genes, and are not brought about by conscious effort.

The human being is different in both aspects. Whereas a person's physical growth comes to a halt in early adult life, there is part of the person that continues growing throughout his lifetime and is brought to a halt only by death or brain deterioration. Secondly, a person not only grows, but develops character, and this development can be guided by conscious effort. Whereas various factors in the person's environment can have significant impact on his character, especially those occurring in early life, the human being is capable of significantly modifying his character (to enhance or weaken his moral and ethical nature), and therefore bears the ultimate responsibility for being whatever he is.

These two features, development of character and ongoing growth, are thus uniquely human features and are thereby components of the *spirit*. *Spirituality* demands that one continue to grow and improve one's character.

Improvement of character is contingent upon one's being aware in what ways one's character is defective, and this in turn is dependent upon a thorough self-analysis. Anyone familiar with the Twelve Steps of the various anonymous fellowships will readily recognize that these components of spirituality can be achieved by the fourth, fifth, and sixth steps:

Step Four: *Made a searching and fearless moral inventory of ourselves;*

Step Five: *Admitted to God, to ourselves, and to another human being the exact nature of our wrongs;*

Step Six: *Were entirely ready to have God remove all these defects of character.*

The requirement that one be fearless in making a moral inventory indicates that there is something very frightening about this chore. Most people will respond that one must be courageous in order to confront the many misdeeds and the less-than-commendable thoughts and acts that are certain to be revealed by a thorough soul-searching. While there is some truth to this, it is not the full explanation.

A moral inventory is analogous to an inventory that one would do of a business concern. What merchandise is on hand, and what merchandise is lacking? What are the concern's assets and what are its liabilities? An accurate inventory requires looking at both the positive and negative.

Discovering unknown assets and abilities within oneself should be an exhilarating experience, much like finding a hidden treasure under the floorboards of one's home. Yet there are people for whom such a discovery poses a threat, and for whom an inventory may be frightening not because it may reveal liabilities, but quite the contrary, because it may reveal the unknown assets that have been lying dormant and unrecognized.

Some people have a pattern of beginning a venture, bringing it almost to fruition, and then doing something to precipitate its failure. Whereas they certainly have a desire to succeed, the additional responsibilities and stresses that success is certain to bring can overwhelm the desire for success, and make failure the easier course. As unpleasant as repetitious failure may be, it has the redeeming feature that one may say, "Don't expect anything of me. I am incapable of doing things right." There are people with a negative, distorted self-image whose feelings of incompetence and inadequacy make success a formidable challenge.

Self-improvement, an important component of spirituality, requires that one have an accurate assessment of one's potential. Such an awareness will not allow one to "copout" and hibernate in a rut. Potentials that are not expressed demand to be actualized, and indeed produce distress if they are not actualized, much as a nursing mother may experience some pain if her infant does not take the milk that she has to give.

Some people may live a long life without ever having been aware of their potential and without having fulfilled themselves. They may even amass great wealth, and may be considered by others to be eminently successful. Yet, their failure to know themselves and to cultivate their potential is a dereliction of their uniqueness as humans. Amassing wealth is not a uniquely human trait, since squirrels hoard more nuts than they can consume, and other animals are also known to accumulate what is wealth for them. The human uniqueness is not an acquiring from without, but in maximizing that which is within. This is an essential of spirituality.

Is not all this emphasis on self-awareness likely to result in a self-centeredness, in a total preoccupation with the self as that about which the entire universe revolves? Will this not bring about an exaggerated importance of one's self?

Quite the contrary. It is only the full knowledge of the self that can bring about a healthy self-effacement, which is the substance out of which virtuous humility can develop.

There are people who are vain, who seem to be totally absorbed with their own importance, and who appear, like the mythical Narcissus, to be in love with themselves. In-depth analyses of these people invariably reveal their grandiosity to be a desperate defense against underlying feelings of worthlessness, and indeed the magnitude of their grandiosity is directly proportional to the intensity of their feelings of worthlessness.

People who feel good about themselves do not need to be constantly reminded how good they are. It is only when one is tormented by feelings of worthlessness that one seeks to escape from them by constantly being reassured that others do esteem him. It is ironic that psychology has applied the term "narcissistic" to these people, because although their behavior appears to indicate that they are absorbed with self-glorification, the fact is that in contrast to Narcissus, who loved himself, these people actually despise themselves. Their self-deprecation is a result of a distortion of self-perception. People see themselves as worthless, and correction of such a concept of self would allow them to dispense with the desperate defense of grandiosity.

One does not really have an option whether or not to have

a self-image. All humans have a self-concept. The only option is whether to have one that is accurate or one that is distorted.

Thinking poorly of oneself is not a virtue. Virtue is truth, and there is no virtue in denying the reality or the truth about oneself.

A proper adjustment to reality can only be achieved when reality is correctly perceived. A person of average income, who deludes himself that he is a multimillionaire is inevitably going to have problems. A person who is in fact a multimillionaire and has the delusion that he is a pauper is equally maladjusted. Just as one must have a valid concept of one's external reality, so one must have a valid concept of one's internal reality. One must know what one's positive components are in order to cultivate them and develop them to their fullest, and one must know one's weaknesses in order to correct them and improve upon them, as well as to protect oneself again challenges directed at one's vulnerabilities.

Just as a person is generally not aware of his throat until it becomes inflamed nor of his ears until they begin to ache, so one is not conscious of the self unless it is ill. Ideally, a healthy person is not self-conscious. A true self-awareness will result in neither vanity nor self-centeredness, but to the contrary, is necessary to avoid and overcome vanity and self-centeredness. It is also essential for the self-fulfillment requisite for spiritual growth.

In the pages that follow, we will focus on some of the features unique to human beings that we can discover in ourselves if we look for them. We will see that these can be developed and nurtured, but that unless we make the necessary effort, they will remain dormant or may even atrophy.

There is no question that virtuosos such as Vladimir Horowitz or Jascha Heifetz had enormous innate talent, yet they spent many hours each day practicing on their musical instruments to attain even greater perfection of performance. Indeed, they never abandoned their quest for improving their skills, or said, "What need is there for improving my skills when I am already recognized as the world's finest pianist or violinist?"

The unique features that constitute our humanity require no less effort in bringing them to their fullest potential than do our artistic, mechanical, or intellectual talents. The ennobling process of character development comprises spiritual growth.

CHAPTER 6

Awareness of History

What experience and history teach is this—that people and governments never have learned anything from history, or acted on principles deduced from it.

GEORG W. F. HEGEL

Are animals aware of their history? I believe the general consensus is that they are not. Does a descendent of Alexander the Great's horse Bucephalus take pride in the equine heroics of his illustrious ancestor and aspire to similar greatness? Does the descendant of a horse who lost a close race know where his ancestor erred so that he can avoid repeating the same mistake? The correct answer to both questions is obviously, *No*.

We have thus uncovered another unique capability of man, which therefore warrants inclusion as a component of the spirit. *Spiritual man is one who is aware of his history*, and who can therefore aspire to the greatness of his forebears and also avoid repeating their mistakes.

It should be immediately evident how much each person as an individual and humanity as a whole would benefit from this aspect of spirituality. It has been correctly said that the only thing we learn from history is that man has never learned from history. How much tragedy and suffering could be avoided if men would only learn from the past.

History is replete with repetitious blunders. As someone remarked, "The trouble with our world is not that 'It's one thing after another,' but that it's the same damn thing over and over again." Things were bad enough when people fought one another by throwing heavy boulders and utilizing primitive weapons. With nuclear weapons at its disposal, mankind's failure to learn from history has become an extremely serious problem in that man now has the capabilities to render mankind extinct.

The two simple words, "I'm different," indicate a blindness that may explain man's avoidance of history. Most people are not foolish enough to jump off a tall building and attempt to fly by flapping their arms. They respect the lessons of the past that teach that everyone who has tried to do so has fallen to his death. Nevertheless those same people see themselves as different and immune to the lessons of history. Therefore, when it comes to building empires, seeking domination over others, or appropriating the property or rights of others, they wear blinders, for history has clearly shown that such acts are futile. Yet, people continue to blunder in their ignorance, deluded by the conviction that, "I'm different," and refusing to abide by lessons easily available in any library in most countries and languages.

In the microcosm of the recovering alcoholic, the failure to respect history and to think, "I'm different," is an inevitable prelude to relapse. We now have documented and verified evidence that once a person has developed the disease of alcoholism, there is no way he can ever return to normal or safe consumption of alcohol. Yet even people with substantial intellectual achievements to their credit, who would qualify as superb human beings by the criterion of their level of *sapiens*, fall prey to the error of thinking: "But I'm different."

Relapse into alcoholism or other chemical addiction may occur in persons whose college degrees and academic honors attest to their intellectual superiority. They may have a period of abstinence during which they appear to have an awareness of the treachery and ruinous consequences of addiction. Their resorting once again to the use of dangerous chemicals leaves us with the conclusion that in spite of their intellectual prowess, these people have not learned from history, namely, the history of their own experiences. To the degree that a person does not learn from history, he is derelict in this unique human feature, which is a component of spirituality.

The lack of this ingredient of spirituality, in which the ego inhibits one's learning from history, is closely related to another aspect we discussed earlier, freedom from domination by internal drives.

Why is it that people who are otherwise capable of making reasonable judgments, who would not be expected to repeat acts that have proven to be self-destructive, are unable to see the obvious? Why do they delude themselves into believing that they are different and that they are immune to the inevitable consequences of such behavior, as history has so abundantly demonstrated?

The answer is that just as a judge's capacity to judge fairly is impaired by a bribe or other personal interest, so is one's own judgement capacity impaired by the self-interest of wishing to gratify one's needs and desires. If a person is offered participation in a business venture of questionable ethics, and there is a great deal of money to be made, it is surprising how many ingenious rationalizations he can produce to justify the questionable ethical practices. We are rarely at a loss for reasons to legitimize something that we strongly desire.

Inasmuch as our internal drives are never completely sub-dued, the only safeguard against being duped by our rationali-zations is to ask for advice and guidance from someone we trust and whose opinion we respect. It often takes an objective observer who is not biased by our personal interest to render a proper judgement. People who adhere to a twelve-step program know that recourse to a sponsor for guidance is indispensable. People who seek spirituality would do well to follow this example and avail themselves of competent counselors to help them avoid the entrapment when a strong desire clouds the truth and prevents them from learning from history and making just decisions.

CHAPTER 7

Purpose in Existence

All men should strive to learn before they die what
they are running from, and to, and why.
JAMES THURBER

Another thought that I am certain never occurs to animals is,
"What is the purpose of my existence?"

People who do not have a belief in God will take issue with
me at this point, claiming that I am now identifying spirituality
with religion, because speaking of a purpose for one's existence
presupposes that there is some ultimate purpose in existence of
the entire universe, a universe in which a human being has an
individualized role. Hence there must have been some Intelligence that brought the universe into being, which speaks for
the existence of a Creator. In a universe that came about
spontaneously out of nowhere and happened to evolve in such a
manner that after billions of years man appeared on this insignificant speck of dust called Earth, man can hardly be considered to have a purpose.

You will note, however, that I did not make it a condition of spirituality that man must *know* his purpose in existence, rather I said that it is unique to man to *think* about a purpose of his existence. If one should come to the conclusion that he has no purpose in existence, it is his privilege to think so, but as a human being he must exercise this unique capacity to at least *contemplate* whether there is a purpose in life or not. True, my religious beliefs have provided me with a sense of purpose. In accepting that there is a God who brought the world into being and created man, I believe that there is a purpose for me in the Divine scheme, and it is my responsibility to seek out and fulfill that particular purpose or mission.

This is of particular importance to me, since I have hypothesized that the presence or absence of self-esteem is the deciding factor in emotional well-being or illness. Self-esteem requires a sense of having value. Generally, we value things for their utilitarian function or aesthetically as ornaments. Since I really cannot see myself as having any decorative qualities, I am left to find my sense of value in answering the question, "What am I for?" To be without a purpose would be devastating to my self-esteem.

But can one have a sense of purpose without postulating a Creator? What about people who are humanists, who believe it is their purpose to promote the welfare of other human beings? Can they not have a noble purpose in life without having a belief in God? Of course they can. Yet noble aims and an ultimate purpose are not the same. An ultimate purpose presumes a reason for living. It triggers action in life to make it all worthwhile. If we have a reason for living we are of value and hence our ultimate purpose is to live a life of value which will affirm that we are here for a reason. Such is the basic tenet of human spirituality.

There is a story of two loiterers who were arrested. When

they were brought before the judge, he asked the first loiterer, "What were you doing when the officer arrested you?"

"Nothing," the man answered.

The judge turned to the second man, "And what were *you* doing?"

"I was helping *him*," he answered, pointing to his companion.

It is obvious that even if one is sincerely helping someone who is doing nothing, the ultimate achievement of both together is nothing.

While helping others is highly commendable, and indeed the world would be a better place if more people were dedicated to helping others, helping others is not the same as having an ultimate purpose. Even if we all help one another, yet do not have something that makes all our existence meaningful, we are left without an ultimate purpose.

But clearly, coming to a firm conclusion about one's purpose and existence is not essential. What is important is that one thinks about it and searches for it. The search is what is uniquely human, and the finding is incidental.

I can respect whatever conclusion a person reaches as a result of this search, but I cannot respect one who dismisses the entire concept of purpose out of hand and refuses to give it any consideration. This is a dereliction of one's capacity as a human being.

In the search for purpose we must be brutally honest and frank. If we are searching for truth, we must be prepared to accept the consequences of truth.

The fundamental difficulty in the search for purpose is that if we do find a ultimate purpose, we feel ourselves committed to fulfill it, and that is indeed a burdensome responsibility. It is much more convenient to avoid the entire issue.

This is the crux of the problem of spirituality. Spirituality and comfort are often at opposite poles. If the way to spirituality were comfortable, most of mankind might have chosen it. It is, however, a long and arduous path, often requiring a basic reorientation of one's character and patience, perseverance, and preparedness for whatever comes.

When I travel through the countryside, I often reflect on the various aspects of spirituality, and it has occurred to me how much calmer and more tranquil life would be if we were free of such turbulent thoughts. Then I pass by a field full of cows, and I see how tranquil they are, lying in the warm sun, chewing their cud. At this point I take pride in being a human being, and conclude that I am willing to pay the price of turbulence rather than be bovinely tranquil.

If there is design and intelligence behind the universe, it is absurd to assume that contentment and tranquility are the goals of life. If the latter were true, there would be no need for the enormous mental capacity that man has.

One of my teachers pointed out that if you were to see a child wearing trousers that are far too long, a jacket whose sleeves extend far beyond his hands, and a hat that comes down over his eyes and nose, you would certainly not conclude that these clothes were designed for him. He has obviously garbed himself in clothes designed for a grown-up. Similarly, if life's aim was to achieve tranquility and contentment, there would be no need for man's mental faculties. The goals of tranquility and contentment are far better served by instinct. Although cows lack color television, sophisticated computers, and the ability to investigate other planets, they are far more content than the wisest human. Man's enormous mental capacities were clearly not designed for the goal of tranquility.

If all life consists of is working all day, then sitting in a bar for hours, or coming home to sit in front of the television until overtaken by sleep, then man's capacity for abstract thinking, meditation, and philosophizing is a complete waste.

We come again to the phenomenon where the tendency to gratify our physical desires may distort our ability to reason properly. Our physical desire is for comfort and tranquility, and satisfying this desire is certain to be frustrated when one searches for purpose in life. The natural inclination is therefore to rationalize and thereby dismiss considerations of spirituality as being irrelevant to daily life. One may reinforce this attitude by invoking the authoritative pronouncements of some respected scientists who contend that whatever cannot be demonstrated in the laboratory is of no value, and because spirituality is not subject to test tube verification, it is a meaningless concept. Such considerations and arguments are nothing but defensive techniques to allow one to remain unperturbed. If one indeed values truth, one should be willing to make the sacrifices necessary to investigate it.

CHAPTER 8

Respect for Others

People who do not experience self-love have little or no
capacity to love others.

NATHANIEL BRANDEN

The individual freedom that is so essential to spirituality cannot
be one's exclusive privilege. To be spiritual, one must respect
others' rights to the same degree of freedom. If we offend
someone, injure him, or deprive him of something that is
rightfully his, we have encroached upon his freedom and upon
his rights. This spiritual aspect of recovery is addressed in steps
eight and nine of the Twelve Steps.

Step Eight: *Made a list of all persons we had harmed, and
became willing to make amends to them all.*

Step Nine: *Made direct amends to such people wherever
possible, except when to do so would injure them or others.*

Unless we make the necessary amends for violating the
freedom of others, our spirituality is lacking. Furthermore,
respecting others' freedom means that we must refrain from
trying to dominate and control them.

Exerting or attempting to exert control over other people, whether overtly or covertly, is one of the most frequent sources of interpersonal problems, and is replete with internal contradictions and irrationality. Some people resent being controlled, yet not only allow themselves to be controlled, but actually invite it. Others deny that they are trying to control anyone, and point to their utter passivity in a relationship, but are not aware that passive-aggressiveness is the most insidious and difficult type of control to identify and remedy.

What is even more confusing is that some people try to control by allowing themselves to be controlled. It is like the mouse in the experimental psychologist's laboratory who remarked to his comrade, "I've really got that guy conditioned. Every time I push this lever, he throws me a food pellet." Little do people realize that trying to control is ultimately futile, and contrary to the opinion of the one who believes he is in control, it usually backfires. Control problems exist, to some degree, in every problematic relationship. However, the whole control issue stands out in bold relief in the family of the alcoholic, and this can be used as a paradigm for all other relationships. To begin with, the practicing alcoholic believes himself to be in control of his drinking, although it is abundantly evident to everyone else that he has absolutely no control over the alcohol, and that to the contrary, it is alcohol that is controlling him. People in the alcoholic's life are under the delusion that they can control him, and are constantly thinking up ingenious new methods to curb his drinking. In spite of the fact that all previous methods have failed, they continue to search for a method that will work, and that will enable them to be in control. The alcoholic, on the other hand, often has everybody dancing to his tune, and far from being controlled, he is actually controlling others because they must adapt to his behavior. It is a well-established fact that when everybody stops trying to control everything and everyone else, recovery usually occurs.

The drive to control others does not necessarily derive from hostile sources. To the contrary, it often stems from a genuine desire to help, as when parents wish to direct their children away from mistakes they themselves have made, or when a spouse wishes to prevent the partner from self-destructive acts, as may occur in the family of the alcoholic. Yet even when the intent is benign, it is important to remember that power corrupts, and that what begins as benign and genuine concern may be transformed into an authoritarian type of domination. Not infrequently the attempt to control is not benign even to begin with, but is merely cloaked in an altruistic garb. "I am only doing this for his own benefit."

It may be difficult to see through the delusions of control. Perhaps if this were possible, reasonable people would relinquish this futile effort. The problem is that for a time, at least, we may assume that one can be in control of others, and this is a difficult attitude to shed.

For example, parents believe that they are in control of their children, at least in adolescence. Certainly the tiny infant is helpless, and is under parental control. The parent places him wherever he wishes, feeds him whenever he decides to, and wakes him from sleep or puts him to bed at whim. The parent understandably assumes that as long as the child is dependent upon him, he is in control.

A bit of observation will reveal the true state of affairs to be different. If one studies a mother feeding an infant of several months of age, one will witness an interesting scene. The mother may be frustrated to discover that the infant clamps his mouth shut when she approaches with a spoonful of food. She then tries to distract the child with some type of toy or activity that fascinates him, and when his attention is diverted and he opens his mouth, she manages to insert the spoon. The infant realizes he has been had, and then sits with a morsel of food in his mouth, refusing to swallow it. Again the mother resorts to ingenious devices to distract the child, and this usually results in the morsel touching the back of the pharynx, which initiates the swallowing reflex. This battle of wills continues so that what could be consumed in less than five minutes is prolonged into a thirty-minute ordeal.

Lest one think that the infant's resistance is due to his simply not being hungry, we need only see what happens if the mother is called away and leaves the food within reach of the infant. The infant eagerly tries to eat the food, and although much of it is spread all over his face, some does reach his stomach. There is no question that what is transpiring is a power struggle, with the mother trying to make the child eat, and with the child resisting being controlled, even if it means that his hunger remains unappeased.

When the child realizes that he invariably loses on the battlefield of feeding, he resorts to his next line of defense, the control of his excretions. It is as he were to say, "You win the battle of getting it *into* me, but I am in control of when to get it *out*." The struggle over toilet training should convince even the most ardent skeptic that the issue at hand is one of control. The child is seated on the mini-toilet, and the mother pleads with him to perform the desired act of excretion. She sings, acts, and bribes, all to no avail. Again, lest anyone think that the child simply does not have the physiological need to excrete at that time, it is only necessary to observe what happens when after half an hour of futile cajoling, the child is removed from the toilet and the diaper is reapplied. Excretion invariably occurs within moments, thus leaving no question that what was going on was a battle of wills.

The dependent child soon realizes that discretion is the better part of valor. There are many things that he desires, and he does not have access to them except through the parents. He therefore decides that it is to his advantage to humor them and give them what they wish so that they will comply with his desires. The child essentially enters into a business deal, and in the back of his head there is the thought that the day will come when he will no longer be dependent on his parents, and he will then do exactly as he pleases. The child understands the terms of this deal, but the parents are deluded into thinking that his compliance with them is a result of his being under their "control."

The delusion of control may have been inadvertently reinforced by modern technology. In days of yore, control was not absolute. The driver of a wagon who wished the horse to turn in one direction would pull the reins, causing the horse some pain that would be relieved only if the horse turned in the desired direction. What appeared to be "control" was actually the horse being put in a state where he chose to produce the desired action in order to be free on pain. This is totally different from turning the steering wheel of an automobile, where there is absolute control by the driver.

We pull levers that move and direct gigantic machines. Little children play with toys that they gleefully direct by remote control. A billion miles distant from Earth a space missile dutifully obeys the orders emanating from the space-control laboratory. In none of these instances do the objects of our commands have an option to refuse. Technology has finally given man a measure of absolute control, and he may think this applies to people as well as machines.

It is difficult to overcome the urge to control when one sees another person, particularly a loved one, behaving in a self-destructive manner. Parents and spouses frequently ask, "How can I stand by idly with folded hands and see him destroy himself?"

The answer is that unfortunately we have no option. All we

can do is advise the person and to the best of our abilities try to impress upon him that his behavior is self-destructive, but beyond trying to convince him to modify his behavior, there is really nothing we can do.

A great deal of anger and resentment is generated when we realize how helpless we are in altering another person's behavior. The "rage of impotence" has almost no parallel in intensity of emotions. Unless we are aware of this and refrain from acting-out our fury, we may do things that are counterproductive and as destructive as the behavior we are trying to control.

Acceptance of this impotence is most difficult. This is where the Serenity Prayer is of such crucial importance. The prayer for serenity to accept the things we cannot change makes us aware that there *are* things beyond our control and that it is fruitless to exhaust ourselves in trying to accomplish the impossible.

From time to time a natural disaster occurs that reminds man of his true state of impotence. It is of interest to observe people's reactions to such happenings. Whereas our ancestors took these things in stride, many people today are incensed by the failure of scientists to prevent the occurrence of such events, and many people look forward to the time when man will triumph over all forces of nature. In an environment where there is a preoccupation with control, it is little wonder that individuals, too, become obsessed with control.

Underlying the urge to control other people is often the distorted self-concept alluded to earlier. People with feelings of inadequacy may attempt to gain relief from these distressful feelings by exerting dominance over others. People who feel comfortable with themselves do not have a need to prove themselves powerful at others' expense. Power-hungry people, whether in the microcosm of the individual and family or the macrocosm of governments of nations are often people whose need to dominate is an unconscious maneuver to overcome their feelings of inferiority and impotence.

The person who feels he is being controlled may react by passive resistance, which is in itself an attempt to control the one who seeks active dominance. This sets up a self-reinforcing and self-perpetuating cycle of action/reaction that is often blatant in families of alcoholics, and often seen in other dysfunctional families.

As a person grows in spirituality, his self-concept improves and he has less need to control anyone else. This not only further enhances his own spirituality, but by eliminating the action/reaction cycle, allows those about him to progress in their own spirituality.

It is clear that the pleasure-producing capacity of any activity should not be the criterion of its desirability. Eating, sleeping, or diversion beyond the point that they contribute to optimum health and functioning are self-indulgent.

A person must work or engage in commerce to sustain himself at a reasonable standard of living. Earning money is necessary for proper living, and can thus be considered a spiritual activity. If the drive to amass wealth exceeds the needs for a standard of living conducive to optimum functioning, it ceases to be a spiritual activity and becomes an indulgence or an irrational obsession.

There is a story of a man who consulted a psychiatrist. "What is your problem?" the psychiatrist asked.

"I don't have any problems," the man answered.

"Then why have you come to consult me?" the psychiatrist asked.

"Because my family thinks there is something wrong with me," the man answered.

"What is it that your family thinks is wrong?" the psychiatrist asked.

"They think I'm crazy because I love pancakes," the man said.

"That's absurd!" the psychiatrist said. "There is nothing wrong with loving pancakes. Why, I like pancakes myself."

The man's eyes brightened. "You do?" he exclaimed. "Then you must come to my home. I have trunks full of them in my attic."

The irrationality here is obvious. Pancakes have value only as a food to be eaten. When one accumulates more than can possibly be eaten and ascribes an intrinsic value to them, we consider this insanity.

There is really no difference in this respect between pancakes and money. If a person tries to earn enough money to live decently and a bit extra to put away for retirement or for unforeseen needs that may occur, this is normal behavior. However, when people already have more than they and their children could possibly consume in two lifetimes, yet continue to amass even more wealth, this is really no different than accumulating crates full of pancakes. Once money loses its utilitarian value and takes on an intrinsic value, its accumulation indicates a lust for power or control, a condition at odds with a spiritual life.

Obviously, animals are not capable of directing their physiologic activities toward any ultimate goal. The animal follows its bodily urges, eating when it is hungry, drinking when it is thirsty, sleeping when it is exhausted, and mating when it is sexually aroused. If a human being does no better than this and performs his physiologic actions solely to satisfy the bodily urges, he has failed to rise above the animal level, and has failed to achieve spirituality. Further, it is evident that spirituality is not solely indicated by prayer, meditation, religious rituals, or even acts of benevolence and charity. Spiritual principles can be practiced in all one's affairs and are evident in human beings who have obtained levels of consciousness beyond animals and have forsaken control for acceptance.

CHAPTER 9

Spiritual in All One Does

> Almost anything you do will be insignificant, but it is
> very important that you do it.
>
> MOHANDAS GANDHI

If one concurs that a human being, in contrast to animals, should strive for something more than gratification of his biologic urges and that he must be considerate of others and not encroach on their rights, one has certainly embraced two important components of spirituality.

Although the Twelve Steps of Alcoholics Anonymous need not be accorded the status of dogma, I have found that they are generally so sound that I am unwilling to dismiss any of them and I have found that each step deserves careful consideration. Hence, when the twelfth step says, *"Having had a spiritual awakening as a result of these steps, we try to carry this message to alcoholics and to practice these principles in all our affairs,"* I pause to reflect, "Why is it important that a person practice these principles in all his affairs?"

Let us take an example of a person who is indeed sensitive to the needs and rights of others and is cautious not to offend or harm others. Let us assume that he has a philosophic purpose in life, and by listening to thoughtful opinions and doing much reading on the meaning of existence, believes himself to be pursuing a spiritual life.

Let us further assume that while this person does not make gratification of his physical desires his *sole* purpose in life, he sees nothing wrong with indulging himself. Although he does not harm anyone with his behavior, he overeats and becomes obese, drinks to tranquilize himself when he feels emotionally uncomfortable, and indulges himself sexually. While his avowed goals seem to meet the criteria of spirituality, it is apparent that this person is in reality a glutton. Is there a fallacy in his reasoning?

This is where the concept of practicing the principles in *all* one's affairs is relevant. Spiritual living does not require withdrawal from life and retiring to a type of monastic seclusion to lead a life of contemplation. Indeed, one can live a spiritual life with involvement in work, commerce, social interaction, sports, recreation, and all other normal activities. However, indulgence is another matter: an overindulgent lifestyle can not coexist with spiritual living.

Let us think of the concept of having a purpose in life as being one's assignment, and compare it to the assignment one is given if one is hired to do a specific task. If I have the responsibility of doing a day's work, I must honestly fulfill this responsibility.

Although my work day may not begin until 8:00 a.m., partying into the wee hours of the morning will so dissipate my energy that I will not be in optimum condition to discharge my duties the next day. I am therefore ethically bound to behave in such a manner *prior* to coming to work so that I will be able to perform optimally.

Although I may be paid for the eight hours of *work*, it is understood that I am entitled to have an appropriate lunch period and perhaps a coffee break, and that the time that I spend eating is not deducted from my pay. Why? Because good nutrition and even a brief break is essential for optimum function, because a hungry worker or one without any break is not as likely to perform as well. If, during the course of my work, one of my tools requires sharpening or adjusting, the time that I spend improving these tools should not be deducted from my pay, because although I was not actually doing the desired work during these minutes, I was engaged in doing something that was essential to the performance of my job. However, if I extend my lunch hour or coffee break far beyond what is reasonable and acceptable, I am derelict in the performance of my work.

The spiritual person who chooses a purpose in life makes that purpose the focus of his life. Of course he must eat and drink, recreate and relax, because these and other activities are essential for his optimal physical and emotional well-being. He partakes of the goods of life to the extent that they contribute to his optimum functioning, but abstains from excesses precisely because they add nothing to his function nor to his goal in life, and indeed, may detract from them.

Is it possible for a person to live his life along such narrow lines? The "Big Book" of Alcoholics Anonymous answers this question in regard to the Twelve Steps by stating that no one is a saint and no one claims perfection. What is described here is the *ideal* for which one should aim in the quest for spirituality.

Unfortunately, some people live their entire lives without giving serious consideration to any of the points we have discussed. Some may even deceive themselves that by following certain religious rituals or going through the motions of prayer they have achieved spirituality, even though they may be inconsiderate of other people and indulge in physical pleasures far beyond that which is necessary for optimum health.

It is not surprising that spirituality's greatest emphasis can be found in the program of recovery from addictions. Many people are swept along by the current of life's activities, and rarely pause to think of what they are looking for. Whereas they may have a number of goals toward which they strive: better job, better pay, greater economic security, a summer home, early retirement, etc., they are not aware that these are but intermediate goals. Indeed, if they were to reflect at the end of the day, week, month, or year, "What have I truly accomplished in this unit of time," they might become upset on realizing the shallowness of their lives. Some people may not come to this realization until their working years are over, and if they then do reflect on what they achieved in their lifetime, they may become depressed.

The alcoholic has an advantage, because addictive drinking precipitates a crisis that requires him to reflect on his life. If he takes the Twelve Steps seriously and realizes the need for pursuit of spirituality, the alcoholism may turn out to be a blessing in disguise. The "rock bottom" experience, the utter bankruptcy of having no other goal than the pursuit of comfort, brings him face-to-face with the meaning of his existence.

This is eloquently stated in the discussion of the sixth step.

In all these strivings, so many of them well-intentioned, our crippling handicap had been our lack of humility. We had lacked the perspective to see that character-building and spiritual values had to come first, and that material satisfactions were not the purpose of living. Quite characteristically, we had gone all out in confusing the ends with the means. Instead of regarding the satisfaction of our material desires as the means by which we could live and function as

*human beings, we had taken these satisfactions to be the
final end and aim of life.*

Bill Wilson, Cofounder of A.A.
Twelve Steps and Twelve Traditions

It would be erroneous to conclude that all recovering addicts
are paragons of spirituality. Many people utilize the recovery
program only to achieve a state of abstinence, and do not
progress any further. Some of these people relapse, some
substitute one addiction for another, and others remain "dry
drunks"; i.e., they no longer drink alcohol, take drugs, or
overindulge in food, but do little to improve their personalities
or to rid themselves of character defects.

The twelfth step refers to a "spiritual awakening." (Step
Twelve: *Having had a spiritual awakening as the result of these
steps, we tried to carry this message to alcoholics and to practice
these principles in all our affairs.*)

The term is well chosen. When one is awakened, one can
either get up and get on with the activities of the day, or turn
over and go back to sleep. A spiritual awakening is no guaran-
tee of a spiritual life. It is only when one adopts the Twelve
Steps sincerely and practices these principles in all areas of one's
life that the awakening leads to growth and spirituality.

I tell people coming into treatment, who invariably feel that
addiction is the worst calamity that could have befallen them,
that they should consider themselves fortunate. People who are
not addicts or who did not "hit rock bottom" may not have
suffered as much, but neither did they have anything to shake
them up and make them take an accounting of what their lives
are all about.

Spirituality is not a "thing," not an object that can be
identified as something one possesses. It is a *process*, a growth
experience. Ironically, when someone thinks he has achieved

spirituality, he has probably lost it. One has it only as long as one is striving for it. Because we can never quite achieve perfection, we are always capable of improving ourselves. As long as we continue to improve ourselves along the lines we have discussed, we are *spiritual*. If we lose the momentum for growth and become stagnant, baser human inclinations toward gratification and comfort are certain to arise and work against the spiritual life. In spirituality, *the searching is the finding, and the pursuit is the achievement.*

CHAPTER 10

Time

Time is nature's way of keeping everything from happening at once.
ANONYMOUS

Time is a spiritual concept.

Animals have biologic clocks, with seasonal and diurnal rhythms that regulate their lives. However, a conscious concept of time is uniquely human.

Since a spiritual life is one that is goal-directed, time has an enormous value. Just as an employer would not tolerate an employee idling away his time instead of doing what he was hired to do, so one who conceptualized his life as being for a purpose should not tolerate wasting time that could be used in furtherance of that purpose. In a spiritual life, time is a precious commodity, and it must be recognized as an irreplaceable resource.

This is not to say that one may not enjoy a long hike in the woods, a fishing trip, or watching a ball game. When activities of rest, relaxation, and entertainment are allocated an appropriate portion of one's schedule they are ingredients of a spiritual life. This idea is contained in the adage, "All work and no play makes Jack a dull boy." Because dullness is counterproductive and inhibits one's performance, activities that eliminate dullness are commendable.

However, indulgence in diversions beyond the point of enhancing optimum function detracts from spirituality. When people find time is heavy on their hands and they look for ways to "kill time," it is indicative of a lack of spirituality. No one in his right mind would willingly destroy something of value, even though it might be replaceable. Why then should people be heedless of time, an irreplaceable commodity? Why let time pass or "kill time" to a degree that is unhealthy? Such is the style of an idler or a lazy person. And laziness is not rest or relaxation.

Relaxation can provide one with a good feeling and a preparedness for optimal functioning while laziness invariably causes dejection, as one recognizes that his time was spent for naught, and thus it deters from optimum functioning. Laziness is a character defect whose elimination is essential for spirituality.

The tendency toward laziness may be very powerful, and the realization that laziness is a character defect often leads one to rationalize and disguise laziness in a fashion that makes it appear more acceptable to the conscience. This is nothing but self-deception.

The ingenious rationalizations that have been fabricated to explain laziness are legion. One wakes up a bit late in the morning, and realizes that it would take extra effort to get someplace on time. Rationalization steps in and says, "There is no point in hurrying. Traffic is so congested that you could never get there in time anyway." Or, "The business of this particular appointment is not all that important. Besides, last time I was kept waiting, so this time let him wait." There is no dearth of excuses that one can provide for oneself to avoid the diligence that would enable one to be on time.

The problem with rationalization is that one may succeed in deceiving oneself. Whereas deceiving others is morally wrong, deceiving oneself is simply stupid. Laziness is usually self-perpetuating. Failure to get done what needs to be done results in an accumulation of work, and the resistance to tackling this additional challenge is increased, thus generating more laziness. This is further reinforced by the feelings of dejection one feels when things are left undone, and this mood dampens enthusiasm and drains one's energies, thus contributing to a vicious cycle.

Laziness is a trait that can be overcome with determination and an initial investment of effort. For example, a habit of late rising can be broken by forcing oneself to arise early for a consecutive number of days, perhaps 20 or 30. After this period, arising early becomes quite effortless, as the new habit replaces the old. As with many other things in life, a wise investment pays well. A change of habit is not difficult if one thinks of the many benefits that will accrue.

As important as is diligence and the judicious use of time, it is equally important that time, itself, not becomes a terror. As we have seen earlier, enslavement of any kind is antithetical to spirituality, and when one is under the total domination of time, one loses a modicum of freedom that is essential to the spiritual life. The clock, therefore, is a useful and indeed indispensible instrument. As an instrument it should be something that we *use*, not something to which we are totally subservient. It is understandable that much of one's day must be regulated by the clock, and it is also important to be precise. Failure to be prompt for an appointment and causing another person to lose valuable time is tantamount to stealing something from him that cannot be replaced. Respecting deadlines may be necessary for proper coordination of a project. All this notwithstanding, we must avoid being terrorized by time. An interesting discovery was made by two cardiologists who were having their office furniture reupholstered.

"What kind of doctors are you?" the workman asked.

"We are cardiologists, heart specialists," the doctor answered. "Why do you ask?"

"It's strange," the workman remarked, "but all your chairs in the waiting room are worn out only at the front edge."

The doctors realized that their clientele were people who habitually sat on the front edge of a chair. These people are unable to sit back and relax, and are always in a state of hyperalertness and constant readiness. Even though they are likely to spend several hours in the doctor's waiting room, they nevertheless perch themselves on the front end of the chair, waiting to jump up at any moment. Being under such pressure is conducive to high blood pressure and heart disease.

Or suppose that one is en route to an appointment, and is caught in a traffic jam due to an accident. One has the option of seething with rage, or realizing that unforeseen incidents are a fact of life that must be taken in stride, and that one might just as well listen to some good music and make the best of it.

I have advised people that when they are on vacation they should put away their timepieces and not consult the clock unless it is absolutely essential. Eat when hungry, go to sleep when tired, and get up when rested. Some people have confided that without their wristwatch they felt not only naked but also totally bewildered, not knowing what they were supposed to do. This is what is meant by the clock being one's dictator rather than a tool.

Time is precious, and in pursuit of one's goal, must be used judiciously. Laziness is a character defect that should be eliminated, but to be spiritual, one must also be in charge of time and not enslaved by it.

CHAPTER 11

Honesty

Make yourself an honest person, then you may be sure
that there is one rascal less in the world.
THOMAS CARLYLE

After having repeatedly stressed that the uniqueness of humans
resides in those qualities that they alone possess, and that these
qualities comprise the *spirit*, it is ironic that one of the most
prominent components of spirituality is not only present in
animals, but is probably possessed by animals in an even
greater degree. That singular, glaring attribute is *honesty*.

Not being well versed in animal behavior, I cannot state
categorically that animals are incapable of duplicity. After all,
folklore does ascribe cunning and slyness to the fox. But I
believe we are safe in assuming that humans are far more
capable of dissimulation than are animals. Any number of
people who have problems with trust state that they feel much
more comfortable relating to animals than to people, because
the former do not conceal their feelings behind a facade of
words.

Animals have not been taught to be as polite as humans. If they dislike you they will bark or hiss at you, or avoid you altogether. Humans will greet you, shake your hand, smile, and tell you how they have been looking forward to meeting you, yet all the while viewing you with distaste. In addition to the duplicity promoted by social graces, there can be frank deception for ulterior motives, as when one person intentionally misleads another and conceals his hostility behind the most enchanting verbiage.

Obviously, animals have many qualities that humans lack, and indeed, much effort is being expended to decipher and understand some of these skills so that we can emulate them. Typical examples of these are the sonar of dolphins and the radar of bats, both highly sophisticated methods of scanning the environment and navigating within it. We have yet to achieve with our advanced technology the precision that is innate and instinctive to animals. We may consider honesty in this same light.

We often think that we stand to gain by distorting the truth. There may indeed be short-term gains, but over an extended period of time, one is likely to lose much more than one can gain by lying. A quick analysis of what has transpired in government over the past several decades, when elaborate efforts to conceal the truth have toppled administrations and truncated careers, should be adequate to convince anyone that distortion of the truth is certain to be ultimately ruinous.

Here is another instance where the recovering alcoholic or addict has an advantage. The lifestyle of addiction to alcohol or other drugs invariably requires one to lie, deceive, and cover up. A thorough recovery from these conditions requires frankness and honesty. One alcoholic told me of an offer he had to participate in a profitable business venture that required some conniving and stretching of the truth. "Maybe that is an acceptable business practice, and maybe there are some people who can afford to do that. I know that I cannot. If I start these kinds of manipulations, it will take me back to drinking, and I never want to go back there again." Another addict who relapsed into use of drugs confided, "I started my decline even when I was clean. Although I wasn't using, I had started lying. I borrowed money, telling people I had a job beginning next week and would pay them back. I had no job. It was a lie, and that is when my relapse began." Many people in recovery from addiction, because they have experienced the consequences of a spiritual void in their lives, are determined to work toward spiritual growth. People who had not experienced such a crisis may not realize how detrimental lack of spirituality is to their lives.

I must admit that for myself, even religious injunctions against falsehood were not completely effective. There were often rationalizations that appeared to justify occasional deviation from the truth: the classic "white lie." It was only after I became involved in psychology that I came to the realization that lying is as futile as it is wrong.

The human brain is an improvement in many ways over the animal brain because the cerebral cortex is more developed. The primary means of communication for animals is nonverbal. Studies of animal behavior reveal elaborate communication methods that include emission of odors, body posture, sounds, and gestures, which communicate messages from one animal to another, particularly within the same species.

With the perfection of speech in man, we have come to rely so extensively on verbal communications that we have lost sight of the fact that even among humans nonverbal communication exists and is operative. There is abundant data on body language and voice inflections, which are not under conscious control. Even if at the conscious level we transmit only verbal messages, there is a simultaneous transmission of unconscious nonverbal messages that have an impact upon the recipient, although these may be received only at the unconscious level. What all this means is that when one tells a lie, one is communicating two contradictory messages: the verbal message which is the lie, and the nonverbal message which conveys a warning to beware of what is being said. Inasmuch as nonverbal messages are not under conscious control, there is no way to avoid the dual message in a lie. The recipient of the lie invariably becomes distrustful of the person who told the lie, even if he makes a conscious decision to accept the verbal message. Down deep, at the gut level, something tells him that he has been lied to, and eventually this unconscious impression will affect his reactions. This will occur even when the person who is lying has adequate rationalizations for lying.

Simply stated, I stopped lying because I came to the conclusion that lying didn't work.

The sense of relief when one dispenses with all lying is indescribable. There is no need to tax one's memory with "What was it that I told him?" and one avoids the fallacy of defending mistakes. As the tenth step says, "whenever we made a mistake, [we] promptly admitted it." When you stop lying, people learn to trust you, and this is a most gratifying feeling.

Of course, there may be an initial cost in being truthful. One can get away with a lie for a period of time, but if we give consideration to the long-term effect, we realize that lying is ultimately not to our advantage.

The emphasis on honesty and truthfulness in twelve-step programs is thus very similar to the emphasis on abstinence. No one will deny that the use of mind-altering chemicals gives one a short-term relief from discomfort. However, the addict eventually comes to realize that the long-term cost of this temporary relief is unacceptable. In a spiritual recovery, use of chemicals and lying are both abandoned for the same reason.

It now becomes apparent why lying is a prelude to alcohol or drug relapse. It indicates that the person is willing to pay the long-term price for the short-term gain, and this is the nature of substance abuse leading to chemical dependency.

Are there not instances when it is permissible to deviate from the truth? Indeed there are, but they are few and far between, much rarer than we think. We are never at a loss for rationalizations to justify lying, but if we will only be honest with ourselves, we will recognize the fragility of these rationalizations.

Expeditious lying may have become so acceptable that it requires a concerted effort to extirpate this habit. One simple way is to commit oneself to respond truthfully to every question *without giving any thought to one's answer* for a period of 30 days. Make telling the truth a reflex. After one has broken the habit of lying, one is then in a position to make exceptions in those very few instances where deviation from the truth is permissible.

Spirituality is built upon truth and cannot possibly coexist with falsehood.

CHAPTER 12

Anger

Anger helps straighten out a problem like a fan helps
straighten out a pile of papers.
SUSAN MARCOTTE

Management of anger is probably the most difficult emotional
problem encountered in modern life. Referring to our compari-
son with animals, we can see that proper management of anger
is a component of spirituality. Animals do not manage anger. If
they are provoked they respond, and they refrain from doing
so only when manifesting their anger would constitute a threat
to their own lives, as when provoked by a more powerful
animal.

Spirituality does not require repression or denial of one's
anger, because denial is a falsehood, and we have established
that spirituality is based on truth. Feeling anger when one is
provoked is as spontaneous and automatic a sensation as the
pain that is felt when one's toe is stepped on. How one *reacts* to
anger is an issue of spirituality.

There are invalid ideas about anger that circulate among some psychologists. For example, it is presented that anger that is not expressed is a source of neurotic or psychotic symptoms, and the therapeutic implication is that one should freely express one's anger. There is nothing to support this theory. Whereas repression or denial of one's anger may indeed be a source of emotional dysfunction, awareness of one's anger and exerting appropriate control over it is not.

A psychological concept that has had legal implications is that of "irresistible impulse." In many cases, it has been assumed that a person may be so carried away by passion or have been so provoked that he is no longer fully responsible for his actions. Fully responsible or not, he must be accountable for his actions.

Twelve-step programs reject unaccountability. Although it is recognized that alcoholism and drug addiction are illnesses, that there may indeed have been an "irresistible" compulsion to use a chemical, and that under the influence of chemicals one's controls are impaired, there is nevertheless no release from the responsibility for one's behavior. Step Eight (*Made a list of all persons we had harmed, and became willing to make amends to them all*) and Step Nine (*Made direct amends to such people wherever possible, except when to do so would injure them or others*) clearly hold a person responsible for his behavior.

The fallacy of the concept of "irresistible impulse" is related to the designation of man as *homo sapiens*. If people of high academic achievement are irascible, their *sapiens* notwithstanding, they are behaving more like animals than human beings.

If one reflects upon those instances where one has responded with fury to a provocation, one usually regrets having done so. This is evident from the abundant explanation one usually gives for having lost one's temper. If it were indeed an appropriate response, what need is there for all the defenses one offers for the behavior?

All one achieves by reacting with fury to a provocation is obviously the immediate gratification of "shooting off steam," which is later followed by regret for having done so. By now we are familiar with this theme, which is just another manifestation of what is so characteristic of addiction: an immediate gratification for which one pays dearly in the long-term.

Spirituality, being in so many ways the polar opposite of uninhibited emotions, is characterized by sacrificing an immediate, ephemeral gratification for the enduring, long-term gain. This applies to the management of anger as well.

Animals are probably incapable of being considerate. Consideration consists of avoiding acts that are immediately injurious or offensive to someone, and also judging the potential consequences. If the consequences appear to be detrimental to others, the act is to be avoided. Assuming that animals lack the capacity for such forethought and analysis, it is evident that consideration is a unique human phenomenon, making it a component of spirituality.

Reflex actions are not considerate acts. The tap of the knee tendon that elicits a leg jerk is a nerve-muscle reaction that occurs at the spinal cord level, and is not even transmitted to nor processed through the brain. More complex acts may be processed through the brain, but only through those portions of the brain that are similar to the animal brain.

Considerate behavior requires that an act be subjected to analysis by the highest levels of the human brain and mind.

This characteristic of consideration is contained in the ninth step: "*We made direct amends to such people wherever possible, except when to do so would injure them or others.*" Making amends appears to be innocent enough and indeed very proper, yet even such a commendable act must be given careful thought: Is it possible that it could in any way give rise to injurious consequences?

Consideration has particular importance for the person recovering from addiction, because all addictive behavior essentially consists of achieving an immediate gratification with total disregard for long-range consequences. Recovery requires looking at the long-range consequences for oneself, and spirituality requires giving thought to the long-range consequences of our behavior on other people. As such, recovery and spirituality go hand in hand.

Consideration thus constitutes the highest level of responsibility, giving utmost thought not only to the immediate effects of our behavior, but to the long-range effects. Such thought requires time, and necessitates removing oneself from the pressures and pace of daily activities. Quiet thought or unhurried meditation can provide sufficient scrutiny to render one's behavior spiritual.

CHAPTER 13

God as Higher Power

One must not hold oneself so divine as to be unwilling
occasionally to make improvements in one's creations.
LUDWIG VAN BEETHOVEN

At this point I am going to discuss spirituality in the light of a
belief in God. Those who are uncomfortable thinking of a
Higher Power with capital letters and who wish to part company with me at this time are free to do so. However, before you
put this book down, bear with me for just a few more moments.

I have by now been involved to a greater or lesser degree
with approximately 40,000 alcoholics or drug-dependent people. Inasmuch as I do not believe that long-term recovery is
feasible without involvement in AA/NA, I always strongly urge
participation in these fellowships.

I have heard just about every possible excuse for refusing to
attend AA/NA, some of them grossly ludicrous, such as when
a person who has made a public spectacle of himself and whose
drunken behavior has made everyone aware of his deplorable
condition, is reluctant to attend AA because this will expose

him as being an alcoholic. Some people find AA too boring, because "You see the same people and hear similar stories over and over again." Yet the fact remains that sitting in the same tavern night after night with the same people and engaging in the same inane conversation was hardly a deterrent from that practice.

I frequently hear the objection, "I have been to a few AA meetings. That program is not for me. All they talk about is God, and I am an atheist. I don't believe in God, and I cannot therefore go to AA."

These remarks are often made by people who have never given any serious thought to the question of whether or not there is a God. Whereas every person is certainly at liberty to believe or not believe whatever he wishes on this matter, the question of whether or not there is a God deserves at least as much thoughtful consideration as whether or not to buy shares in a particular company, or whether or not to purchase a certain style of shoes. Some people who will do extensive research in business or fashion, for that matter, will dismiss the concept of God without the least bit of investigation. Should they or should they not believe in God is a question that does not arise.

The objection to AA/NA meetings because they are God-oriented is usually not a responsible decision reached after considerable deliberation. It is most often simply a rationalization, a way to avoid the message of AA/NA that one must be totally abstinent. There are avowed atheists who successfully utilize AA/NA without relinquishing their atheism, and there are people who profess deep religious convictions and who are devout adherents of a faith who shun AA/NA as being too secular in its insistence on a loose concept of a "Higher Power."

When someone objects to AA/NA because he does not believe in God, I point out to him that he is actually deceiving himself. "It is not quite true that you do not believe there is a

God. The way I see it, my friend, you *do* believe in God. Your problem is that you think you are Him."

This is more than a wisecrack. Invariably the alcoholic drug addict who rejects the AA/NA program of total abstinence rejects the concept of loss of control. He is fiercely insistent that he has control over alcohol/drugs and of everything else in his life. The idea that he has lost control over alcohol/drugs and that his life has become unmanageable is anathema to him, in spite of the fact that every outside observer can readily see that there isn't even the least semblance of control.

This refusal to consider that one may have lost control and that one's life has become unmanageable stems from only one source: an unshakable conviction that it is utterly impossible for such a state of affairs to exist. Or to put it even more simply, "It is impossible for me to be out of control because I wouldn't allow such a thing to happen." Loss of control is incompatible with omnipotence, which is what such a person assumes himself to be. When one believes that one is omnipotent, he is his own god.

It has been established philosophically that there cannot be two omnipotent beings. If one is more powerful than the other, then the latter is not omnipotent. If both are absolutely equal in power, then one can restrain the other interchangeably, and neither is then omnipotent. Ergo, there can be only one omnipotent being.

It follows that as long as a person cannot accept that it is possible for him to be out of control and considers himself to be omnipotent, he cannot believe in God, because then there would be two omnipotent beings, which is impossible. Hence his only recourse is to deny the existence of God.

My advice to the person who rejects AA or NA because of its espousal of God is as follows: "Let us not even talk about God now. That idea does not even occur until the third of the

Twelve Steps. Let us begin with the first step and admit loss of control and unmanageability. Discard your fantasy of omnipotence. Once you have done that and have admitted that you are not God, you will be in a position to reflect whether there is or is not a God out there."

Therefore, before abandoning the idea of God, give it some consideration. If you were planning to decline an investment opportunity in a company, you would want to know something about the company that justifies your rejection. What does it manufacture or sell? How long has it been in operation? What is its performance record? What are the indications that the company is unstable and therefore a poor risk? Who is recommending this investment? These and other appropriate questions will help you reach what you hope is a proper decision. You would not turn down an opportunity without good cause.

And so the belief in existence or nonexistence of God cannot be reached on whim. It is an issue that can determine the course of one's entire life. Give this issue serious consideration. Read, ask, discuss, and think before you conclude. Recognize that twelve-step groups are for everyone including the atheist. And bear in mind that when people refer to their Higher Power as God, so too, could you.

CHAPTER 14

Divine Providence

One meets his destiny often on the road one takes to
avoid it.

FRENCH PROVERB

Associating with people in fellowships who are recovering from
addiction,* one frequently hears about incidents that are considered Divine intervention or indicative of Divine guidance.
Skeptics are likely to dismiss these as fantasies, and I would
also have done so had I not personally witnessed many such
happenings.

I once sought an appropriate AA contact for a patient in
detoxification, and being unable to think of someone in recov-

---

*In twelve-step fellowships the term "recovered" is avoided, because it connotes
that one has totally overcome the addictive disease, and just as someone who has
fully recovered from pneumonia has no further need of antibiotics, so someone who
is recovered from addiction would no longer require ongoing help. Furthermore, if
one were *cured* from the addiction, one could again use alcohol like any nonaddict.
Since both of these are not true, the term recovering is used to indicate that the
addiction has been arrested and that the person is not actively using alcohol or
drugs, but that he continues to be an addict even after 50 years of abstinence.

ery who lived near this 38-year-old civil engineer. I called a young woman who I knew lived in the south side to assist me in locating someone. I knew that Ursula had been attending AA and was in her second year of recovery. She indeed did contact someone for me, and when I told this to the unit nurse who was a twelve-year veteran of AA, she said, "I hope you talked to Ursula about herself, because she has been drinking sporadically and has been slacking off in her meeting attendance."

I was reluctant to believe that Ursula had relapsed, but when the nurse told me that she was Ursula's AA sponsor. I accepted this disappointing information.

The following day when I called Ursula and thanked her for arranging the contact for my patient I cautioned her: "I also want to tell you, Ursula, that you don't have to go all the way down in order to quit."

"What do you mean?" she asked.

"When you came in for treatment," I said, "you were in the pits. Although you have started drinking again, you don't have to get back to that terrible state. You can stop right where you are."

Ursula began crying. "How did you know?" she asked.

"How I know is totally irrelevant," I said, although I was a bit surprised that she did not realize that her sponsor and I are in frequent contact. "All I am asking of you is that you call your sponsor and get back to regular meetings."

"Okay, I promise," she said. "But I can't understand how you found out."

I then told the nurse that she would soon be hearing from Ursula. "How come you asked Ursula for a south side contact when she lives in the north side?" she asked.

"No way!" I said. "Ursula lives in the south side."

"Don't tell me where she lives!" the nurse said. "I have frequently dropped her off at home after meetings."

It suddenly struck me. "Which Ursula are you talking about?" I asked.

"Ursula Johnson," she said.

"*I'm* talking about Ursula Smith," I said.

"Who is Ursula Smith?" the nurse asked.

I felt a shiver going up my spine. I called Ursula Smith and told her exactly what had happened.

"I couldn't understand how you could have found out about my slip," she said. "After I left rehab, I was sober for over a year, then I drank for two days. I was okay for another few months and again I drank for only one day. This last week I again drank for only one day, but nobody knew about these slips. I hadn't even told my sponsor. It was so weird that you called me, because nobody knew."

"That's not quite right," I said. "Someone *did* know, and that Someone arranged it so that I would call you."

Ursula did return to regular meetings, and is at this point five-years sober. Coincidence? Perhaps.

One time I was traveling to another city, looking forward to taking my new car onto the highway. I had not yet left the city when the speedometer cable broke. With less then three hundred miles on the car. I was not only upset about this inconvenience, but also concerned that I might have acquired a "lemon." After a few blocks I pulled into a gas station to see whether the mechanic could replace the cable. Two men were standing in front of an automobile. The hood was raised and steam was rising from the motor. I recognized one of the men as a recent alumnus from our rehab center.

"Hi, Doc!" he said. "Broken radiator hose. What's your problem?"

"Broken speedometer cable," I said. "Brand-new car, too." I then proceeded to give him a tight hug. While the mechanic replaced my cable, I noticed that my friend was pacing to and fro like a caged animal. Eventually he came over and said, "Can you drop me off nearby, Doc?"

When I told him I would, he told his friend to go on alone.

Once we were in the car, I noticed my friend's forehead to be full of beads of perspiration, and he was visibly trembling.

"You won't believe this, Doc," he said. "I've been clean for four months since I left Gateway. Today Frank came over and asked me if I wanted to go out with him. I was the one that turned Frank on to coke. My resistance broke down, and we were on our way to cop some coke when the radiator hose burst, and then you drove up."

I parked the car and we talked a bit. I then suggested to my friend that I drop him off at a meeting. He is now seven-years clean.

Again a coincidence? Perhaps. But I prefer to believe what one AA member said: "Coincidences are miracles where God prefers to remain anonymous."

Does God intervene in the lives of human beings? Or does the Master of a universe whose expanse is just beginning to dawn upon us have more important things to do?

Astronomers tell us that our planet is a tiny satellite of the sun, and that the latter is probably a less-than-average-size star in our particular galaxy. Our own galaxy is many light-years in dimension, and there are greater galaxies that are billions of light-years away.

A light-year is not a unit of time, but of distance. Because light travels at 186 thousand miles per second, a light-year is the distance that light would traverse in a year, or 5,878,000,000,000 miles! A billion light-years is 1,000,000,000 times that. In this vast space there are an inestimable number of stars, many of which would dwarf our sun. In this whole scheme a tiny little planet is not only insignificant, but of lesser stature than a single drop of water in the Pacific Ocean. This entire enormous universe is the domain of what we may call God, and are we to believe that He is in the least bit concerned with what goes on in the existence of a single person on this less-than-noticeable speck of dust we call Earth? Come now!

The argument is convincing, but the events are even more convincing. Obviously there can be such things as chance occurrences, but one reaches a point where ascribing things to chance or coincidence requires a greater act of faith than belief in Divine intervention.

"But," the skeptic will say, "if there is Divine intervention, why does God seem to restrict his attention to recovering drunks and junkies? Aren't there other people who are at least equally deserving? We hardly hear such incidents reported by other people."

Of course other people have such incidents, and if you ask people who are not in recovery, they can tell you of happenings, in their lives that they ascribe to Divine intervention. However, many people hesitate to talk about such things because in a scientific era, where everything has a logical explanation, it is just not acceptable to talk about such things because someone will accuse you of being "wacky" or of being a religious fanatic. In respectable circles, Divine providence is given lip service, and one goes through the motions of praying to God, but His intervention in one's life is not to be taken seriously. Among many recovering people this taboo does not exist, and they talk freely of incidents where Divine intervention is the only reasonable explanation for what happened.

Most recovering addicts achieve remarkable transformations and refuse to accept the credit for their remarkable changes in values and health. "There is no way I could have done this," is a common remark. "I know that this is the work of God. All that *I* did was get out of His way."

The third step of the recovery fellowship reads, "*We made a decision to turn our will and our lives over to the care of God, as we understood Him,"* and the eleventh step reads, *"We sought through prayer and meditation to improve our conscious contact with God as we understood Him, praying only for knowledge of His will for us and the power to carry that out."* When a person sincerely adopts these steps in his life, he is indeed more likely to interpret chance and coincidence as Divine intervention, whether or not he is an addict, and by so doing he builds upon his faith and his level of spirituality rises accordingly.

CHAPTER 15

Understanding God

It is only by forgetting yourself that you draw near to
God.

HENRY DAVID THOREAU

The phrase "God *as I understand Him*" is a bit tricky. It was
inserted to avoid making the Twelve Steps restrictive and de-
nominational. By adding the qualification "as I understand
Him" it makes the Twelve Steps acceptable to Christians,
Moslems, Jews, Buddhists, and to those who understand their
Higher Power to be something other than a deity, yet who can
use the word "God" as a convenient term to express the idea of
a power greater than themselves.

The tricky part is that if we think of God in the traditional
sense, the Creator of the world, the idea of understanding Him
is untenable, because a bit of analysis will show that God is
beyond human understanding. Indeed, the reason for faith in
God is that logic cannot possibly carry us that far. Faith begins
where logic and understanding end.

There is a popular phrase, "Seeing is believing." Nothing

could be more wrong. Seeing is *not* believing, and indeed believing is in a way the very antithesis of seeing. I do not "believe" that I am holding the pen I am writing with, nor do I "believe" that there is a table before me on which I am writing. I do not "believe" there is a sun, moon, or stars. I can "see" all of these things, and there is no need for me to "believe" that they exist.

Nor do I "believe" that water is composed of two parts hydrogen and one part oxygen, because that can be proven in the laboratory. Similarly, I need not "believe" that when a transversal intersects two parallel lines, alternate interior angles are equal, because that can be proven by reason. Anything which can be demonstrated to the senses or logically proven is not an object of belief.

The very fact that the existence of God is an act of *faith* indicates that His existence can never be absolutely proven logically, and it is advisable to show why we cannot understand God or prove His existence. Our idea of God is that He is the Creator, or as Aristotle liked to say, He is the "first mover unmoved." Assuming something comes from something else, there had to be a "first something" that started it all, and that first something is what we refer to as God. The logical question that every child asks is, "And where did God come from?" to which there is no answer. If you do not assume that God is the first, then He was brought into existence by "something" that preceded Him. Well, it's just a mistake in identification, because that "something" is really God. In other words, we run into the problem of *eternity*, of something being around which had no beginning.

Our human capacities are limited. For example, the human ear can hear only sounds that are within a certain range of frequency. And just as our senses have their limitations, so does our thought. We can understand only those concepts with which we have some contact, some experience. Nothing we have ever come in contact with or had any direct knowledge of has been eternal. The whole idea of eternity frustrates human logic. The atheist, who does not believe in the concept of God because he considers it to be irrational, will have to postulate that matter always existed or that energy always existed. If the universe was not created, as religion teaches, out of absolute nothingness, then it had to come from something, and this something always existed. Belief in the eternity of matter is just as nonrational as belief in an eternal God. If you really think deeply into the concept of eternity, pretty soon your head starts spinning. There are just two approaches to get your head back on track. Either one can say, "Eternity is beyond my ability to comprehend, therefore I must have *faith* in there being an eternal being," or, "Eternity is beyond my ability to comprehend, so I will just dismiss the whole concept and assume that the only things that do exist are those that I can understand." The first is the way of the believer, and the second is the way of the atheist.

Characteristics that believers ascribe to God, such as infinity, omniscience, and omnipotence are equally without limits, and as such are beyond our capacity to understand.

Many contradictions occur when we try to think about God. Generally, God is thought of as *absolute perfection*. Something that is absolutely perfect must be unchangeable, because change is either for better or for worse. Any change would mean that God was more perfect or less perfect before or after the change. This is impossible, because God is absolutely perfect, then there can be no change in God.

If we can conceive of God in understandable dimensions, the logical question is, Why would an absolutely perfect being create a universe? Why would He do anything? Is He any happier having the universe than before? This would mean that

He underwent a change, because He was previously lacking a universe which He now had, and as we have stated, change in God is impossible. Logically, then, there could have been no creation, and the logical conclusion is that because God is absolutely perfect, He never created anything. Nothing exists. It's all just one great big delusion. But as Descartes pointed out, in order for me to be deluded I must be in existence. So *something* does exist, which means that God did create something, which makes absolutely no logical sense.

Alas, thinking about such things leads us into mind games which have no solution. If we make the leap of faith, we say, "I do not understand. Whether or not God exists, the concepts of eternity of time and infinity of space are unmanageable by my human mind, so I cannot understand. The best I can do is understand why I cannot understand. I rely, therefore, on the teachings of my parents and forebears, on the wisdom of some great minds, and in what has been handed down to us from revelation. I *believe* in that which I cannot understand." That is the statement of faith.

This is why "God as I understand Him" is an important key qualification. Due to the limitations of our understanding, God will be constructed by believers in any way they wish. As was pointed out, humility is crucial to spirituality, and what better way is there to achieve humility than to realize how limited even the greatest human mind is and that in this matter of defining God we can be without dogma, allowing for faith only in something greater than oneself. The one requisite is belief. In AA, where for newcomers a belief in a higher power is often impossible, it is sometimes suggested to believe in a light bulb. Believe in an electric current, *but do believe.*

CHAPTER 16

Turning One's Life Over to God

> Many could forego heavy meals, a full wardrobe, a fine house, etc.; it is the ego they cannot forego.
> MOHANDAS GANDHI

Earlier we noted that to live spiritually one must have a purpose in life. For the person who believes in God, that purpose is to fulfill the will of God. Hence the third step refers to turning one's life over to the will of God, and the eleventh step describes the method to discover what that will consists of. Just a decision to go to New York or Los Angeles or Wichita doesn't get one there. One must consult a map or a travel agent for directions.

It should be apparent that the eleventh step in AA (Sought through prayer and meditation to improve our conscious contact with God as we understood Him, praying only for knowledge of His will for us and the power to carry that out) does not immediately follow the third. Those who composed the Twelve Steps were obviously aware that a great deal of work must be done before we can find our way to the desired goal.

There may be many factors that can obstruct or greatly distort the search for the goal, and unless these are eliminated, we may be frustrated to find ourselves at a dead end, or what is worse, we may stray far from the correct course. The intermediate steps, four through ten, are to enable us to search for what is God's will for us.

Turning one's life over to the will of God is not a simple task, and most people find it formidable. We feel secure when our hands are on the steering wheel, and it might seem like stupidity to let go of the steering wheel. The third step can therefore only come after the first two.

Just what can you do if you find that the steering wheel simply does not work, and that regardless of which way you turn the wheel, the car goes its own way? This is a frightening experience, and one can only pray for a miracle and hope that one does not get killed. If one survives, one can take the car to a mechanic to have the steering mechanism repaired.

Alcoholics have a quaint way of expressing things. One alcoholic said, "When I realized the total shambles my life was in, the only sensible thing to do was to fire the guy who was running it." If one comes to the realization that one's life has become unmanageable, it is only logical to try and find someone more competent to manage it. The person who believes in God finds it reasonable to turn his life over to the will of God and lets things happen in God's way and in God's time.

The slogan of the fellowship, "Let Go and Let God," is not really all that radical. One is not required to let go of the steering wheel if the mechanism is intact. It is only when the mechanism is nonfunctional that the slogan "Let Go and Let God" is appropriate. "Get out of the driver's seat" is the customary remark heard in twelve-step programs.

This point deserves emphasis, because some people misinterpret "Let Go and Let God" as meaning that one should abdicate all efforts to do anything. This is not true at all. Do whatever you can do if it has the remotest chance of being effective. However, if the steering wheel has become disconnected from the front wheels, it is delusional to think that turning it is going to be of any value. If one realizes this, then one might think of something else, such as stepping on the brake to diminish the impact of hitting something, or jumping out of the car if that is feasible, or if there is no other option, praying.

The problem many people have is that they do not recognize the analogy. Even when their lives have become totally directionless and they are virtually bouncing off the wall, they delude themselves that they are somehow still in control. As long as they maintain this delusion, they will not seek help elsewhere.

"Let God" does not mean that one should expect one's direction to come from a Divine revelation with a bolt of lightning and clap of thunder heralding a pronouncement from Heaven. God often communicates to us through people. There are many wise and experienced people who can come to one's assistance when one's life has become unmanageable. The problem is that some people, even when seeking advice, may listen to what is being said and then go on to do things their own way. Letting go and letting God means accepting the directions we are given. People in the twelve-step fellowships can attest that when they do this, their lives take a turn for the better.

The difference between just seeking advice and "turning one's life over" is precisely that in the former approach one picks and chooses, and essentially is not "letting go," while in the latter one asks God for guidance, then goes to a meeting and shares his dilemma with those who are there. Although no one is an

oracle, if one believes that the fellowship will be the conduit for
Divine direction, one will accept guidance.

Ask those who have tried it. They will tell you that it
works.

CHAPTER 17

Mastery Over Emotions

Courage is resistance to fear or mastery of fear, not
absence of fear.

MARK TWAIN

Step Six: *Were entirely ready to have God remove all these
defects of character.*

How does one get completely ready? Furthermore, because
character defects include such things as envy, lust, greed, and
hatred, how can one divest oneself of emotions? Being responsible for one's actions is one thing, but achieving mastery over
one's feelings seems to be a bit unrealistic.

To some degree, common sense should be of help. Take, for
example, the feeling of envy. This is not only a morally
reprehensible feeling, but also one of utter futility. Being envious of someone will not give you what he has. Envy's usual
products are tension, aggravation, and high blood pressure.
Even though in some cases envy may drive a person to great
heights, it is simply foolish to harbor a feeling that is so

self-destructive. For an addict, envy can be ruinous and may trigger a relapse.

We are not as helpless in dealing with feelings as we may think. As a rule, feelings developed only in regard to that which is possible, even if only remotely so. Thus, if one were to discover that on a planet of a distant star there are mountains of diamonds, one would hardly give them a second thought. Because there is no way one could possibly reach that planet, there is no point in desiring something that is totally beyond one's grasp. As intense as our desires may be, they are nevertheless subject to this single rule of logic: One does not crave that which is impossible or that which is absolutely beyond reach.

If we find ourselves to be envious, hateful, greedy, or lustful, it is because we have not placed the objects of these emotions absolutely beyond our reach. The objective of hatred is destruction of the despised object, and if we hate someone or something, it is only because somewhere in the recesses of our conscious mind there is a connivance, however subtle, that we can in some way settle the score. If we were determined that come hell or high water we were not going to act on our hostility, the feelings would decrease and eventually be dissipated.

This is true of all other emotions as well. One would not lust for the impossible, nor covet something that he knows he cannot get. For one to be free of an undesirable emotion, it would be necessary for him to be absolutely determined that he would *never* acquire the particular object that triggers the emotion, nor take any unacceptable action toward that object. Regarding the object as being absolutely beyond one's range should essentially eliminate the emotion.

I must take issue with a fundamental Freudian principle. Freud postulated that *all* dreams are desires for wish-fulfillment, and must be analyzed and understood in this context.

I think it is possible for dreams to be beyond wish-fulfillment. One can dream of total absurdities and only ingenious casuistry can interpret such dreams as desires for wish-fulfillment. One can indeed wish for something highly improbable, but whereas one can *dream* of the truly impossible, one does not *wish* for the impossible.

The reason for the distinction between a wish and a dream is that dreams originate from the *unconscious* mind, and the unconscious is not bound by reality or the laws of logic, as Freud correctly pointed out. A *wish*, however, is a conscious phenomenon, and the conscious mind does comply with reality. If reality dictates that something is absurd, one may still "dream" of it, but one would not *wish* it.

We are held accountable for our conscious thinking, and not for our unconscious thoughts. To covet is to consciously wish.

It is no coincidence that the commandment "Thou shalt not covet thy neighbor's wife or belongings" is preceded by "Thou shalt not murder, Thou shalt not steal, Thou shalt not commit adultery, and Thou shalt not bear false witness." If one is truly committed to avoiding unjust aggression or taking another's possessions, it is possible to refrain from coveting.

If one has indeed done one's homework in getting "ready" to rid oneself of character defects, yet finds that some objectionable traits remain, one is then in a position to petition God to remove the remaining vestiges. As with anything else, we cannot expect Divine assistance until we have first done all that we can do and should do ourselves.

Getting one's emotions under control and ridding oneself of character defects is no small task. Taken on alone, it is not only formidable, but may be well nigh impossible. What makes the task feasible is the conjoint efforts of the many people in the anonymous fellowships who share the same burden and are working toward the same goal.

In order to enhance character building, one should avail himself of one or more people whose love, honesty, confidence, and unrestrained frankness can be trusted. To such a person, one can entrust one's innermost feelings, and from such a person one can expect an objective judgment. Through another's eyes you will see yourself in a different light, even if this judgment is skewed. For in discovering the error in judgment about oneself made by another person, one may actually discover things about oneself that would otherwise not have been detected. Getting to know oneself through someone else is essential to self-awareness.

People who have not rid themselves of character defects often find it difficult to become part of the group. Their apprehension that their deficits will be discovered results in their forming only superficial relationships. The advantage of the twelve-step fellowships is that one quickly discovers that one is not unique, and that many other people are struggling to overcome those very same defects. Frustrations with life's circumstances, annoying personality traits as well as serious problems with character are shared in a twelve-step fellowship.

Finally, we will always maintain our separateness as people, but such separateness is primarily a physical separation, because it is our bodies that remain distinct and unfusible. Spirits are not constrained by boundaries of space, and spiritual people can fuse with one another to truly share their strength, hope, and courage, and thereby make the eradication of character defects feasible.

CHAPTER 18

The Will of God

It is my earnest desire to know the will of Providence
in this matter. And if I can learn what it is, I will do it.
ABRAHAM LINCOLN

A scenario: "OK, God. I give up. My life is a mess. Help me
out of this."

The Divine response to this is, "Of course I will help you.
But first you have to discontinue messing things up, otherwise
it will be like trying to bail out the boat when the water is
coming in faster than you can get it out."

"But I'm not drinking or drugging anymore, God. What else
do You want me to do? What other things am I doing that are
destructive?"

Says God, "Sit down and make a list of everything you have
done, then get someone to go over this list with you to help
you to discover what parts of your behavior are constructive
and which are destructive. Then I want you to correct things
you have done to others by compensating them for any harm
you have done to them, asking their forgiveness, or both. Keep

on the alert for repetition of any destructive behavior, and if it occurs, don't be obstinate in defending it. When you've done all this, come back to me and I will be glad to help."

This Divine response constitutes Steps Four through Ten.

Why is making a moral inventory so essential before trying to learn God's will? Because until we have done so, our character defects of lust, greed, envy, resentment, and egocentricity are so likely to influence our thinking that we are apt to conclude that the will of God is what *we* want. History is replete with all kinds of immoral and unethical acts that have been done in the name of God. We can only arrive at what is truly God's will if we eliminate the personal interests that are the products of our character defects.

"But all that is going to take time, God. I'm in trouble now, deep trouble. I need help now. I can't wait!"

What is the Divine Response? "You never were able to wait, were you? Don't you see that this impatience and wanting a quick fix is a character defect you must get rid of? Instead of working things out, you used to reach for a drink or a drug because they worked fast. For you fast is destructive. You think that by stopping the use of chemicals you have solved all your problems, but as long as you're still looking for the quick fix, you really haven't changed much. Now that you have decided you want spirituality, you want instant spirituality. Well, there is no such thing as instant spirituality."

"But I'll tell you what," God continues, "you just begin working on changing yourself, and try sincerely to correct those character defects, and I'll help you. But no bargaining, no trading this for that. Your efforts at improving yourself must be sincere."

"OK, I'll begin. But what's in it for me, God? What do I get out of all this?"

"What's in it for you?" God responds. "You're back to

square one! You said you were willing to do *My* will. The right question is not 'What's in it for me?', but 'What is it that God wants?'"

"OK, I'm game. What is it that You want from me, God?"

"It's simple," God says. "I sent the message through Micah (6:8). 'What is it that God asks of you, but to do justice, love acts of benevolence, and walk humbly with your God.'"

"Is that all there is to it, God? I thought it was much more complicated."

"No, it is not at all complicated. Keep it simple. But even though it is simple, it isn't easy. It will be a struggle, a continuous struggle, and sometimes even a more difficult struggle as time goes on. You see, I created you with some very strong biological and emotional drives, and it is my will that you become master of these drives. These three things, doing justice, loving benevolence, and walking humbly are often antagonized by these biological drives that always wish to gain the upper hand. You will be surprised to discover how your personal interests can twist and distort what is justice and what is benevolence. Your ego will fight ferociously to prevent you from being humble. It is your job to prevent your baser drives from gaining the upper hand."

"But what's the point of all the struggle, God? Why did you create me in such a fashion that my entire life must be a struggle?"

"You would like to understand it all, wouldn't you? I cannot blame you for that. But just think, if you understood it all, and if everything I wanted you to do was perfectly logical, then you would be doing it because you understood it. You would then be following the dictates of *your* mind, and not submitting to my will. The only way you can be obeying My will, is if you do *not* understand.

"The one thing you *should* understand, is that I do not stand to gain anything from your submitting to my will. I lack for nothing, and there is nothing that you can give me. It should be apparent to you that even though it is my will, it is all for *your* ultimate advantage."

Doing the will of God may not be easy, and turning one's life over to His care may seem foolish if not ruinous, but if we are to achieve a spirituality that involves God, we must be ready to follow him and place ourselves in His care.

CHAPTER 19

Does God Care About People?

A man's heart considers his way, but only God lets his
step reach the aim.

PROVERBS 16:9

Turning my life over to the will of God means that He has a
will for me, something that He wants me to do with my life.

How can God possibly be interested in the actions of a lowly
human being? Haven't we pointed out how negligible and
infinitesimally small our Earth is in the immense universe? Why
would God pay any attention to something so trivial? Would it
not make more sense if God restricted His attention to much
greater things, such as the movements and functions of galaxies
that span distances of thousands and millions of light-years?
Assuming that humans are too trivial to be deserving of Divine
attention, wouldn't it be more appropriate to say that God
takes interest in the majestic heavenly host?

If we but remember that God is infinite, we can see that there
is nothing either too trivial or great enough to warrant Divine
attention.

When you say that something is trivial, it is always on a comparative basis. A cupful of water may be a trivial amount relative to the vast amount of water in the Pacific Ocean. But to the amoebae, paramecia, and other microscopic protozoa, a cupful of water is like an immense swimming pool, indeed, a whole lake.

You can speak of something being big or small if it is in reference to something finite. For example, a twenty-five-cent piece is of some significance relative to a dollar, because it constitutes a fourth of a dollar. When compared to the national debt, however, a quarter is insignificant, because it is only one-fourth of a trillionth of the national debt, hardly a significant sum. A sum of one hundred billion dollars, however, is significant when compared to the national debt, because it represents a tenth of that amount, which has relative significance. The great discrepancy between a twenty-five-cent piece and a hundred billion dollars, however, is only when both are compared to a finite sum, like the trillion dollar national debt. Compared to *infinity*, however, both are equally significant or equally insignificant.

What is one divided by zero? Infinity. What is .00001 divided by zero? Infinity. What is 1,000,000,000,000 divided by zero? Infinity. Infinity is without dimension and limitation, hence *relative to infinity* large and small are equal in magnitude.

Relative to God, who is infinite, the greatest of galaxies and the most prominent of the heavenly hosts and the smallest of humans are all equally significant or insignificant. God is either interested in everything or in nothing. It is therefore possible to believe that God is interested in the universe He created, and in the lives and actions of an individual human being as well.

We most often assume that a major hindrance in spirituality is the lack of a strong belief in God. The fact is that more often the problem is a lack of belief in *oneself*. Some people fall into a rut of despair and self-deprecation. What difference does it make whether I am drunk or sober, using or clean? No one really cares. I don't have the strength or willpower to resist the addiction. Why should God take an interest in whether I stay clean or sober or not?

Belief that God is in charge of the world means that He is in charge of my very being. If He did not want my existence, I would not be existing. He must have some reason for wanting me to exist. There must be something that I can accomplish with my life. Furthermore, that particular "something" cannot be accomplished by anyone else in the world other than myself, because if it could be, then there would not have been any need for me. I am unique and I am important.

Self-awareness and self-appreciation of what we are is neither vanity nor egocentricity. These are crucial to spirituality, because they give us a sense of duty and responsibility.

One time I interviewed a young woman who had been severely addicted to drugs. Her hands and arms were scarred with tracks where she had injected drugs into her veins, and there were also residual of abscesses due to infections of the injection sites.

I noticed that the young woman was wearing a golden locket, and at my request, she took it off and handed it to me.

As we continued talking, I picked up a sharp instrument and acted as though I were about to scratch the locket.

"What are you doing?" the woman asked.

"Nothing much," I answered. "I'm just going to scratch this up a bit."

"Why do you want to do that?" she asked.

"Because I like to," I answered. "It gives me a kick to scratch things up. What difference does it make to you."

"Don't do that!" she said. "That's mine, and it's very beautiful and valuable to me!"

"Just let your ears hear what you have said," I said. "If something is beautiful and valuable to you, you are careful to not let it be damaged. Now look at your arms. If you felt beautiful and were valuable to yourself, this never would have occurred."

A self-awareness that we are children of God, and the true conviction that we are precious will militate not only against self-abasement by drugs and alcohol, but also against any other behavior that diminishes us.

The reason we should abstain from wrongdoing is not only because it is morally wrong, but because we should be so occupied in the pursuit of fulfilling our mission in life that we should simply not have free time to squander on activities that are not directed toward this goal. If we realize the importance of our fulfilling the mission that God has for us, we will dedicate ourselves to discovering just what that mission is. The biblical formula is indeed simple: Do justice, love acts of benevolence, and walk humbly with your God.

But what is justice? Is it just that some people suffer poverty without an opportunity to extricate themselves while others are born to luxury and excess? Is it just to allow people to be homeless if there is a way of providing shelter for them? Is it just to be cruel or abusive to others, or to allow such practices to continue when we could take remedial action? Ensuring justice is not the sole prerogative of the legal system, but the responsibility of everyone. Hence, we must be aroused to do whatever is within our means to bring about true justice and by so doing ennoble ourselves as caring, spiritual human beings.

One who truly loves acts of benevolence pursues them with the passion of love. Too often people discharge their responsibilities to the less fortunate by writing a check to a community agency, thereby appeasing their consciences that they have done their share. Never mind that many community agencies are woefully understaffed and underfunded, and cannot provide the proper care for the aged, the infirm, the neglected, the dependent and abused children, and the homeless. Are we or are we not our brothers' keepers?

Justice and benevolence are not only topics for social policies and practices. Right in the midst of our own homes and with our own family members there is need for justice and benevolence. Some people are tyrants within their own homes, trying to dominate and control other members of their families. Such behavior is neither just nor benevolent.

Walking humbly before God requires humility, and true humility may well be the key to ridding oneself of all character defects. Humility would prevent us from holding grudges, because this is invariably the result of feeling that one's honor was offended. Humility would eliminate the need for us to be critical of other people, because who are we to pass judgment on others? Humility would eliminate greed and envy, as we would be satisfied with what we have, and not aspire to fame, wealth, and power.

These three characteristics, cited by Micah, are the three fundamentals for fulfilling the will of God. It is the task of the spiritual person to study them and observe them to the utmost.

CHAPTER 20

Man's Will vs. God's Will

> Although the world is full of suffering, it is also full of
> the overcoming of it.
> HELEN KELLER

One of the obstacles in turning one's life over to the will of God can best be expressed, "But what happens if His will doesn't coincide with my will?" This takes on an even greater significance when we raise the objection that God has allowed so many terrible things to occur. "How can I trust Him with my life?"

A rather sarcastic answer to this question would be, "Well, then don't. Just trust yourself. But if you are someone who has made a total wreck out of your life, would it not be wiser to set aside your infallible judgment?"

Yet, it is not quite fair to dismiss a legitimate question with a sarcastic answer. The fact is we frequently do observe things happening that cause much pain and suffering to apparently innocent people. God permits these things to happen. Every thinking person has asked, "Why do bad things happen to good people?"

Let me first tell you my answer, and then we will discuss it a bit. My answer is, "I don't know."

When innocent people suffer as a result of the actions of other people, the question is somewhat less challenging. One of the areas of conflict between some schools of scientific psychology and theological psychology is that of determinism vs. free will. Some psychologists, Freudians among them, contend that man really is not a truly free agent, and that his behavior results from the interaction of his internal impulses and various external conditions that impact upon him. They contend that man's consciousness of his behavior gives him the illusion that he has free will, but that his behavior is in fact determined.

If a person's actions are all determined, then there can be no such thing as virtue or sin. Creatures that operate according to fixed natural laws are neither moral nor immoral. It is natural for a hungry lion to be a predator and kill for food, and he is driven to do so by his biologic impulses. The predatory behavior of the lion is thus really no different than the destructive eruption of a volcano, because they both operate according to immutable laws of nature.

Judaeo-Christian theology, however, teaches that there is indeed such a thing as virtue and sin. Although a human being is motivated by internal drives and influenced by various external forces, he is nevertheless ultimately responsible for his behavior, and it is he who makes the final decision whether to act or not to act in any specific way.

The concept of virtue and sin, which is central to Judaeo-Christian theology, is thus predicated upon human free will. It therefore follows that although God is omnipotent and can control everything, He has left the area of moral choice, the decision whether to act in a good or evil fashion, to man himself. For whatever reason God has left man to choose between good and evil, it is essential that man be free to do so, for otherwise it is not a choice. Just as a tree that produces fragrant blossoms and delicious fruit cannot be considered virtuous, nor a bush that produces sharp thorns or toxic berries cannot be considered sinful, neither could a person be considered virtuous or sinful unless he is free to choose his behavior.

The consequence of this system is that because God delegates to man freedom in his moral actions and does not intervene to stop him from sinful behavior, it is possible for an innocent person to become the victim of someone's evil behavior. Thus, if a person decides to burglarize someone, and God does not intervene to stop such sinful behavior, the person who is burglarized may therefore suffer, although he is not deserving of punishment.

Is this fair? Many of us would agree that the suffering of the innocent is most unfair. And further, is it not totally unfair that a person whose mother's drinking during pregnancy resulted in fetal damage must go through life suffering from physical deformities and mental retardation? The person who is born with deformities is the innocent victim of someone else's improper behavior. While we indeed perceive such happenings to be unfair, we can at least understand how it is that innocent people may bear the consequences of other people's behavior.

But what about earthquakes, floods, and tornadoes that are in no way the result of human deeds, and in which innocent people are the victims? What about incurable diseases that strike good people, young and old? What about crib deaths or children born with some physical and mental defects that are not the result of parental neglect or abuse? How do we logically square these away with the belief in an omnipotent, benevolent God?

I don't know, although there are some people who seem to

know everything. Such people can tell you that a natural tragedy that took many lives and inflicted much suffering was a Divine punishment. "God was giving those people their just desserts for their sinfulness." This is not only stupid, but cruel as well. What man can claim that God has taken him into His private counsel and revealed why He allowed certain things to occur? It is nothing but the grossest arrogance and vanity to presume to understand the mind of God. Furthermore, to tell people who are in distress that they are being persecuted for their sins is the height of inconsideration, and indeed is outright cruelty. It is pouring salt on open wounds. If one has nothing comforting to say to people who are suffering, one should remain silent. Reasonable people simply admit that they do not know and do not understand, and make themselves available for any help they can provide in any way possible.

Every once in a while we can gain a bit of insight. I recall one woman who related some of the disasters that befell her during her drinking years. "When I lost my job, I was devastated. When my marriage broken up, I felt it was the end of the world. I was angry at God. 'Why are You doing this to me? What did I ever do to You to deserve this?'"

"Now I am seven years sober," she said, "and I can see that this was God's way of taking away from me those things that I did not have the good sense to give up myself.

"I can see now that I was in a sick marriage. I am now in a much healthier relationship. I am about to get my master's degree, something that would never have happened had I stayed at that job."

So there are incidents where the passing of time shows that God was right and we were wrong. But there are so many others where, try as we might, we cannot come to any reasonable explanation, and we must admit that these are beyond our comprehension.

Some people have solved the dilemma by postulating that God has simply abandoned the world or has lost control of it. If this were so, it would be meaningless to turn one's life over to the will of God or to pray for Divine guidance. Assuming that God has not abandoned the world and does maintain control over everything except for the area of free moral choice which he has delegated to mankind, leaves one with the conclusion: I do not understand.

This conclusion need not be a threat to anyone's ego. Far greater minds have wrestled with the problem of the existence of evil and suffering, and have eventually come up empty-handed. The scriptural Book of Job is a very profound and comprehensive discussion of the enigma of why the innocent suffer, and fails to come up with a logical explanation. After all attempts at explanation fail, God says to Job, "Where were you when I created the universe?" In other words, "I have a master scheme for the entire universe, and in this scheme each piece of the puzzle has its proper place." Questioning any single event in the entire series of events in the universe is like picking up one or two pieces of a million-piece jigsaw puzzle, and after examining them closely, saying "I don't see the picture."

Why do we continue to turn to God for help after He has allowed us to suffer? The only answer I have to this came to me in a pediatrician's office.

A mother had brought her infant to the doctor for the second or third of a series of injections to immunize him against whooping cough, lockjaw, and diphtheria. When the baby saw the doctor clad in white, he began screaming, remembering only too well what had transpired on his last encounter. The baby clung to the mother, and when the mother tried to restrain the infant so that the doctor could administer the injection, the baby began clawing, kicking, and biting the mother. She was now the enemy, collaborating with the vicious assailant who was about to stab him with the needle. Once the injection was over and the doctor left, the baby once again clung to the mother for dear life. This scene was very revealing to me. The infant, totally incapable of understanding anything about being protected from devastating diseases, perceived the process as an assault against him. The mother's collaboration with the assailant left no question but that she had turned against him, and he therefore attacked her. Once the painful episode was over and the mother released her restraint, the baby recognized her as his protector, as his life's source, and turned to her for relief.

This is how we may sometimes relate to God. When we are in distress, our anger at God may be aroused, and we may express ourselves harshly toward God. We may rest assured that God understands this very well, and does not love us any less for our attitude than the mother who is the recipient of the infant's hostility when she restrains him for the doctor. But after the particular incident is over, we turn back to God for support and protection.

Being angry at God is not at all blasphemous. Reflect for a moment. You cannot be angry at something that does not exist. Anger at God is a very positive statement of one's conviction that God exists, and is merely an expression of sharp disagreement brought on by distress. As one wise man said, "You can be for God or you can be against God. You just cannot be without God."

The acid test of faith is primarily the weathering of adversity without losing trust in God, and the ability to accomplish this is a major step in spiritual progress.

CHAPTER 21

Patience and the Ultimate Goal

> All human wisdom is summed up in two words: wait and hope.
>
> ALEXANDRE DUMAS

Patience and perseverance.

Many people have television sets that are "instant on" models, where the picture appears the moment the set is turned on. Old fashioned sets require warm up time. How long is the wait? Approximately twenty-five seconds. If we prefer sets that eliminate the twenty-five-second waiting period, how can we talk about patience being a virtue, and especially, how can we ever hope that our children will value patience?

In a culture that knows no patience, the addict (alcohol, drugs, food, etc.) is the personification of impatience. Suppose I were to offer addicts a drug that produces the most intense "high" at an absurdly cheap price. Without doubt, the supply would rapidly be exhausted. The following day all the customers would accost me, enraged that I deceived them, because the drug had no effect whatsoever. "Oh, I'm sorry," I say to them,

"I neglected to tell you there is a lag of forty-eight to seventy-two hours before the 'high' comes on." I am certain that I could not sell a single dose after that. Even the most intense high is of no use to the addict unless it comes on quickly.

In recovering from addiction, the addict must overcome this trait and learn patience. This is encapsulated in the slogan, "Time takes time."

One of my most cherished letters from a former patient reads as follows:

> *It was four years ago this week that I was brought into your office, utterly beaten, wanting to die but lacking the courage to take my own life. It was only through your persistent urging and offering of hope that I followed through with AA.*

> *The only thing I did right those first two years was not drink and go to meetings. I want you to know that it took four years for me to feel differently about myself. I don't have to tear myself down anymore. I don't have to keep myself sick anymore. I am so grateful to God, the program, and the people.*

This woman felt that the first two years were but a latency period, and that nothing of substance was occurring. Obviously, this is not true. In addition to changes that certainly occurred but were not evident to her, the very fact that she could persevere in absence of perceptible change is in itself a major achievement and a reversal of her intolerance of waiting and frustration during her active addiction. Perseverance is one of the most difficult challenges for the recovering addict. Success in persevering is contingent upon another characteristic of spirituality, that of purposefulness.

Purposefulness requires a single-mindedness. Everything one does or does not do must be subordinate to the overriding motif of one's life. This concentration on living with a purpose enables one to break through the most difficult obstacles.

The potency of the laser beam demonstrates the enormous force that emerges when all phases of light are converged into a single beam. The phenomenon of the extraordinary strength of karate is another example of what can be achieved when all energy is concentrated on a single point. We learned of this phenomenon as children when we used a magnifying glass to focus the sun's rays, setting fire to a piece of wood or paper.

Is it possible to achieve this single-mindedness, yet live a normal life? Would not one have to retreat to the confines of a monastery or otherwise seclude oneself from the distracting turmoil of daily living in order to concentrate all one's attention on a single motif?

No such isolation is necessary. Think of the mother of a small infant, whose overriding interest is to care for her child's needs. She goes about her daily activities in the household, reads, watches television, and converses with her friends while the baby is resting or asleep. However, the moment the child makes the slightest sound indicating that he may need attention, she responds immediately. Why? Because the infant is never outside of her thoughts. Even while she is engaged doing other things, and her conscious thoughts are otherwise occupied superficially, the infant is always with her, and she never puts him out of her mind for even a second. This is even more pronounced in the hypnotic sleep of a nursing mother. Her sleep is so profound that even an explosion would not arouse her, yet just the slightest grunt by the infant brings her to full alert.

An enormous force of good, like a laser beam, can pierce barriers. The latter are the myriad distractions that occur when we dissipate our energies in various directions without having even an approximate goal for our lives. Strange that people may carefully schedule their vacation days, giving much thought to all that they wish to see and do during this period of diversion, yet allow themselves to drift aimlessly through their entire lives, with no sense of direction.

A plan for life is essential. One can go about one's daily activities, giving them their due attention, while never losing sight of one's ultimate goal in life, which should pervade all of one's activities, if not consciously, then in the immediate preconscious. This single-mindedness can bring about the perseverance necessary to reverse a pattern of living that has been deeply ingrained for decades, and allow the emergence of an entirely novel personality.

CHAPTER 22

Peer Pressure

Do not follow the multitude to do wrong.
EXODUS 23:2

There is one trait in animals that has its analog in humans, but unless the two are distinguished and seen only as analogous and not simply identical, there is a risk of serious consequences. The uniqueness of human beings within the animal kingdom allows for freedom from primordial instincts and this uniqueness qualifies it as an element of spirituality.

Animals have a herd instinct. How is it that one small lad can lead a herd of hundreds of powerful oxen? Because each ox thinks that several hundred other oxen are driving him. The herd instinct has been well documented, as when animals band together for either offensive or defensive operations.

When the herd instinct functions among humans to unite them for offensive or defensive actions, it may be constructive. However, when the herd phenomenon displaces individual judgment, it can be most destructive. Many young people have entered into the lethal cycle of addiction as a result of peer pressure, surrendering one's judgment to the group.

We have every right to champion the cause of democracy. In the final analysis, democracy has proven itself to be the most equitable and just form of government. Yet, majority rule has its limitations. Morality is not subject to majority rule.

When some states voted to retain slavery, this did not make the enslavement of a human being any less immoral. The morality or immorality of the United States' involvement in Viet Nam is debatable, but whether or not the majority of the elected representatives of the populace voted to support the action is not the determinant of its morality. Similarly, the vote of a duly elected legislature to legalize prostitution would not affect its morality. Society calls for a code of morals and ethics from a higher source than the will or whim of a legislative body.

The message of the scriptural story of Noah is precisely that one individual may be virtuous in defiance of the corrupt values of his entire culture. Those who worship at the shrine of democracy should not lose sight of this.

The mentality of those who see majority rule as the criterion of right or wrong is reflected in the repetitious arguments for legalization of something or other. Without entering into controversy, it is important to remember that a legislative vote on whether anything is legal or illegal, be it gambling, prostitution, abortion, use of drugs, or euthanasia, has no bearing whatsoever on whether it is morally right or wrong.

A spiritual person must be a moral and ethical person. Moral and ethical values should be established in the home, and this is primarily a parental responsibility. If one fails to exercise one's inalienable right to establish spiritual standards of right and wrong independent of public opinion, one should not be surprised if one's children succumb to peer pressure and use drugs because "everyone else is doing it." Preaching values will have no impact. Living according to one's principles and sacrificing for one's beliefs and principles is the only hope of providing children with the necessary fortitude to resist peer pressure.

CHAPTER 23

Prayer and Faith

Many things are lost for want of asking.
ENGLISH PROVERB

Step Eleven: *Sought through prayer and meditation to improve our conscious contact with God as we understood Him, praying only for knowledge of His will for us and the power to carry that out.*

For those with faith, prayer is an essential ingredient of spirituality.

The concept of prayer is frequently misconstrued. Many devout people pray regularly, yet may be missing the essence of prayer.

Some people pray the way a child begs its mother in a toy store or candy shop. "Mommy, buy me this. Mommy, can I have that? Mommy, if you buy me this, I will be good forever. I will always finish everything on my plate and go to sleep early and I will never hit the baby. Please, Mommy, please, can you buy me that?"

There's really nothing wrong with this kind of prayer. In fact, it is quite commendable that a person feels himself to be a child of God, and does not hesitate to ask God for anything and everything. Sometimes people are reluctant to ask God for things that are trivial, as though He should only be approached for major things, and not be bothered with relatively unimportant things. In a child-parent relationship, a child does not hesitate to ask the parent for anything and this is how we should relate to God. The only drawback of this kind of prayer is that it does not go far enough.

But let us examine this type of prayer a bit. We should remember that when we pray for something we want, we are *asking*, not *commanding*. Some people become disillusioned if they do not get what they pray for, and conclude that prayer is ineffective or that God is not listening. This is a distortion of prayer, because it is as if one were telling God what to do, and He is supposed to obey. Instead of a person understanding that he is supposed to do the will of God, this attitude is just the reverse: God is supposed to do the will of man.

While it is important to realize that God may respond positively to our prayers, we sometimes fail to recognize this, as in the story of the very devout man who climbed to the top of the roof to escape the rising waters of a flood, and prayed to God to save him. Looking for a direct sign of God's help, he refused the help of boats and helicopters to rescue him, although three times they came to assist him, and he ultimately drowned in the flood.

In Heaven he approached the Divine throne, and complained, "God, I always trusted in you, and I prayed to you to save me. Why did you let me down?" To which God responded, "You fool! I sent three boats and helicopters to save you!"

Sometimes we have our own ideas just how God is supposed to fulfill our requests, and if things are not forthcoming exactly the way we would like them to be, we assume that God is not responding to our prayers.

I am certain that a small child who is denied ice cream just before her meal feels that the parents are being unreasonably cruel. Her juvenile mind cannot grasp that it is not to her advantage to have sweets before a meal. The child knows only what she craves, and the parents' refusal to satisfy that craving may cause her to be angry with her parents and accuse them of not loving her.

But if God will only give us that which is for our own good and deny that which is detrimental for us, why then should we pray at all? Why not just leave everything to God's judgment and not bother asking him for anything? Why pray at all?

Rather than informing God of what we want or need, the purpose of prayer is peace of mind. It is a way to turn our needs and drives over to a Supreme Bring, and thereby lighten our own burden.

Similarly, the hymns of adoration of God are not for God's benefit. He does not have to be reminded of His greatness, and He is not in need of our praises. The adoration of God is to remind *us* of His omnipresence, omnipotence, and omniscience. The adoration of God is a way in which we keep our faith in Him alive.

We do many things in our lives, and it is our obligation to do what we must. "God helps those who help themselves." However, we go through many motions, and it is a mistake to think that we can control outcome, and it is important that we recognize that we are responsible for what we *do*, but we are not responsible for what results.

In much of our lives, especially in economic affairs that occupy so major a portion of our lives, what is good and what is bad (and indeed right and wrong) are generally determined by outcome. If a person makes a foolish investment or starts a business venture with reckless abandon, yet circumstances occur that make his investment or venture phenomenally successful, it will be said that the investment or venture was a *good* one. On the other hand, if he had made a very careful and thorough study prior to investing, and was most cautious in planning his business venture, yet the results were financial failure, it will be said that the investment or venture was *bad*.

In the sphere of commerce, where profit and loss is the criterion of success or failure, it is understandable that the focus must be on outcome. However, in our personal lives, good and evil, right and wrong, must be determined by *how we arrived* at a decision and what motivated us to act in a particular manner. The physician who maintains a high standard of excellence and who treats his patients sincerely and with the sole consideration of doing what he feels is best for them is not at fault if a treatment fails. The physician who does not care about the welfare of a patient, and who chooses a particular form of treatment only because he can make more money is unethical, and is to be condemned even if the treatment fortuitously succeeds.

I have seen parents who bear eternal guilt because their children grew up to be criminals, addicts, or otherwise dysfunctional. Very often these parents were not neglectful and did their utmost to provide for their children both materially and emotionally, yet in spite of their efforts, the children grew up impaired. On the other hand, there are parents who lived dissolute lives and grossly neglected their children, yet their children grew up to be model citizens. Morally, the former parents are deserving of praise and the latter of condemnation, although if one were to judge by the outcome, the reverse would apply.

We are not prophets. We can only do what we consider to be proper and right, and allow ourselves to be guided by ethical and knowledgeable people. Often, how things turn out is out of our hands. Yet, we are so prone to thinking that we *are* in control, that it is necessary to remind ourselves through prayer and meditation that we are but a part in a process and that we do not control the outcome. What we have is faith: we have faith that if we do our part to the best of our abilities, the outcome will be the right one.

Returning now to the problem of unanswered prayers, we should realize that God's bounty emanates from Him, and that we must make ourselves suitable recipients of that bounty.

If one has a radio that produces annoying static instead of beautiful music, one should not call the station and complain about the poor quality of their broadcasting. Rather, one should have the radio repaired so that it can properly receive the radio waves. So it is when we are recipients of the Divine bounty. If our lives are full of static, we would do well to investigate what we must do to improve *ourselves*, and not attribute the problem to God.

When we pray sincerely, and recognize the majesty of God, we are motivated by faith to exert ourselves toward a life of human dignity and worth. In doing so, we improve and refine our character, and as with the radio set that is repaired, the static is replaced by beautiful music.

We can now understand why praying for others is particularly important. When we pray sincerely for other people, we set our own personal interests aside, and are considerate of the needs of others. This certainly contributes appreciably to the refinement and improvement of one's character.

The eleventh step elevates the concept of praying to new heights. *"We sought through prayer and meditation to improve our conscious contact with God as we understood Him, praying only for knowledge of His will for us and the power to carry that out."* Note that there is no mention of a prayer for fulfillment of one's desires, but for improving one's relationship with God. This is prayer at its finest.

Prayer is a vehicle for bringing man closer to God. The highest aspiration a person can have is to stand in close relationship to God. When this is the intent of prayer, it indicates that one has risen far above one's personal interests, and that the latter have been displaced by the desire to be close to God.

The human being is a composite being, consisting of an animal body and a Divine soul. Just as the body component requires of a source of energy—calories and essential minerals—for its existence, function, and growth, so does the soul require its particular nutrients.

We may conceptualize the soul as being analogous to a photoelectric cell that is energized by the rays of the sun. Exposure to the sun increases the energy of the cell, and lack of exposure depletes it. Similarly, the exposure of the soul to God increases its strength and vitality.

We can have faith that prayer is the vehicle whereby the soul is brought closer to God. Sincere prayer brings the person into a direct communion with God. Having a faith of this magnitude produces its own energy and propels the faithful toward a richer and nobler life.

A number of years ago, I prayed at the Western Wall in Jerusalem, and I thought that the attitude of my prayer was quite good. Then I saw a blind man being escorted to the wall. I watched as he touched the rippled stones with his hands, feeling centuries of history at his fingertips. Then he gently bestowed a kiss upon the wall, and began his prayer.

This prayer was not a psalm, not a hymn, and not anything of the established liturgy. It was an intimate communication, and I watched and listened as he spoke informally to his God, variously relating things that had happened, and asking God to bestow true peace upon mankind. At one point he stopped abruptly and said, "Oh, I'm sorry. I already told you about that yesterday," and then continued on.

As a man of faith, I was electrified by this apology. Here was someone who was speaking to God directly, and upon recognizing that he had repeated what he had already said yesterday, apologized to God just as one would apologize to another person for taking up his time unnecessarily. This man had no doubt whatever that God had heard him yesterday. But his apology for saying something that was unnecessary had the irrefutable implication that all else that he said *was* necessary for God to hear, and that he felt it was important for him to relate this to God. I then reflected that I had not even begun to pray properly.

Praying for the knowledge of the Divine will for us is edifying, because it reinforces the conviction that one has an important function in the universe. In contrast to the prayer for things that we ask from God, which is our awareness of things *we need*, this prayer for knowledge of His will for us is an assertion of our awareness that *we are needed*.

Again the genius of the authors who compiled the Twelve Steps is evident because it is not until after the eleventh step that they refer to a "spiritual awakening." It is through prayer, and particularly through prayer for the knowledge of God's will for us and the ability to fulfill that will, that we come to a true spiritual awakening.

As we mentioned in an earlier chapter, when one's body is deprived of its essential nutrients, we develop symptoms and sensations of discomfort of one type or another. When our soul is deprived of its essential nutrients, we will also develop symptoms, a vague feeling of discontent, as though something is wrong but we are unable to put our finger on just what that something is. Too often people turn in desperation to various behaviors that will deflect this feeling of discontent, such as ingesting chemicals that will anesthetize them so that they feel nothing.

The needs of the body are finite. We need just so many calories, just so many minerals, and just so many vitamins. We need just so much rest and just so much diversion. This is clearly a case where more is not better, because an excess of food and certain vitamins and minerals can produce serious physical consequences. The needs of the soul, however, are infinite, and the source for satisfying those needs too, is infinite. It is prayer that joins us to the Infinite.

CHAPTER 24

Inability to Pray

Often our trust is not full. We are not certain that God hears us because we consider ourselves worthless and as nothing. This is ridiculous and the very cause of our weakness.

JULIAN OF NORWICH

But what if we try to pray and cannot? What if we find ourselves thinking, "I am a phony. I pray *this* way, but I live *that* way." Do not be discouraged. You are probably being more honest than many other people.

To a panel of rabbis at a weekend gathering on spirituality, one woman expressed her distress. "I walked by the synagogue this morning, and there everybody was praying. I wanted to go in, but I couldn't. I have tried to pray, but I just can't seem to make it."

I was asked to respond. "I am simply amazed," I said, "by your interpretation of what is and what is not prayer. Your perception was that I was praying and that you were not. But let us look at it from God's perspective. When He sees me walk into the synagogue, He probably says, 'Oh, here comes Twerski again. What is it that he wants *this* time? He is always so self-centered. God, give me this, give me that. Always give me!'"

"Then God sees you standing outside the synagogue, wanting to enter, but feeling unable to pray. 'Now there is My child who would like to get close to Me, but is frustrated because she does not know how to do so. Her prime wish is to be able to pray!'"

"Now tell me," I said, "whose prayer do you think God prefers? My 'gimme' prayer or your silent prayer to be able to pray?"

The most sincere prayer does not always emanate from people who appear to be most devout. At one AA meeting, an alcoholic with six years of sobriety told of his years of unsuccessful battle with alcohol. Ultimately he came to the conclusion that if he were to recover, it could only be with the help of a power that was mightier than both he and alcohol together. "I concluded that I must try and look for God. I visited churches, synagogues, and various religious institutions," he said, "but it was all in vain. I could not find God anywhere, and I came to the conclusion that it was all a myth, and that there was no God.

"One day I was walking along the seashore," he continued. "I had nowhere to go, having been thrown out of my own home. I looked up at the sky and shouted, 'Well, if You're there and You can hear me, then help me!' and He did."

I know there can be many psychological explanations for this man's life taking a dramatic turn at this moment of desperation, but I am a simple person, and I can accept very simple and obvious explanations. This man had turned to God in utmost sincerity, albeit with much doubt, and his rather unusual prayer was answered.

As far as considering oneself to be a phony, I can only comment that no phony has ever even considered the possibility that he may be a phony. Questioning one's own sincerity is a sign of honesty.

There is yet another obstacle to prayer, and ironically, it is that the prayer might be answered. There is a witticism among twelve-step programs, "Be careful what you pray for, because you might just get it."

Our lives are fairly well immersed in the pursuit of nonspiritual goals: wealth, fame, and gratification of our physical desires. We pray for enlightenment, for God to show us His will, and give us the strength to carry it out. But do we really mean it? What would happen if we were to achieve the Divine enlightenment for which we pray? Are we ready to surrender all the physical comforts we enjoy and our various mundane aspirations if these are not God's will for us? Is our prayer not more apt to be, "Look, God, I am saying this because it is the right thing to do, but please don't take me seriously"?

If you happen to feel this way, do not let it stand in the way of praying. Keep trying. There is truth in the suggestion, "Fake it until you make it." This is not being hypocritical as long as you are aware what it is you are doing and not deceiving yourself.

One does not become a violin virtuoso overnight. It takes many hours of dedicated practice, and the novice violin player does not produce beautiful music. Like so many other things, prayer takes practice. Keep on saying the words. Eventually they will have their desired effect.

CHAPTER 25

Contrition

When I listen to my mistakes, I have grown.
HUGH PRATHER

In twelve-step groups character refinement is contingent upon several important components of the steps: an inventory, frankly admitting one's defects, ridding oneself of these defects, and making amends. Obviously, without a knowledge of one's defects, no corrective action is possible.

There is, however, a pitfall for which one must be on the alert. Whereas awareness should lead to constructive corrective action, it may produce a detour into remorse, and this can be a costly deviation.

I would like to define terms. The term "remorse," as used here, refers to self-pity. It stands in sharp contrast to "contrition," when one is aware of wrongdoing and takes corrective measures to right matters or at least prevent a recurrence of past blunders, hurts, or simple mistakes. "Remorse" on the other hand consists of feeling sorry for oneself and wallowing in self-pity.

It is easy to mistake "remorse" for "contrition," but the two are poles apart. Veterans in the recovery program know that when one is displaying "remorse" or feeling self-pity, the next drink could be close at hand.

We have already established the importance of self-esteem in spirituality, and it is again of crucial importance here. If one has an expensive garment that becomes stained, one feels badly that this has happened, and takes the proper steps to have the stain removed and restore the garment to its original beauty. Indeed, one would pick and choose to make certain that one employs the finest cleaner who will remove the stain carefully, so as not to do damage to the delicate garment. If, on the other hand, the garment is a worthless rag which has little value, one may not even bother to have it cleaned, and just dispose of it. Certainly if one were to make an effort to have the latter cleaned, one would hardly select the most skilled craftsman. One might even try to remove the stain oneself, using harsh chemicals that could ruin the garment, because it really does not matter that much.

Similarly, if one values oneself, discovering a blemish on one's character will stimulate one to take the necessary steps to remove it carefully.

A spiritual life should be an enjoyable one. As one veteran of AA said, "If you are not enjoying sobriety, you are doing it wrong."

Character improvement can be hard work, but by no means does this preclude enjoying it. Someone who thoroughly cleans his home may have to exert himself quite strenuously, but the knowledge that the house will be clean allows him to enjoy what he is doing, the hard work notwithstanding.

There are people who ruminate over the past and become fixated on mistakes they have made. Their demeanor is dejected, as reflected in their somber facial expression, slowness of activity, lack of initiative, and morbid attitude. It is easy to assume that this remorse is a sincere regret for the past and a sign of one's spiritual values, but nothing could be further from the truth. The essence of a spiritual life is to fulfill one's mission in life, and when one is in a state of inaction, paralyzed by depression, one can accomplish nothing.

There is a difference between recalling one's mistakes and obsessively ruminating about them. There is the story of a person who was lost in a forest who, when he retraced his steps on a path that did not lead out of the forest, would make a mark on a tree to indicate that this was one path that he should not try again. This is the sole purpose of remembering what one has done wrong: to avoid repeating mistakes. Making amends wherever possible is responsible behavior and the only decent thing one can do, but brooding over past mistakes does not accomplish anything for anyone.

We have already noted that it is important to give up the delusion of control. Sensible thinking will lead to the obvious conclusion that although we can often make amends, the past cannot be undone. What possible purpose can there be in ruminating over the past? It is evident that rumination is really only an extension of the delusion of control, where the individual refuses to relinquish the past, and is preoccupied with the thought that *he could still change it*. Brooding over the past is nothing more than an absurd belief that one can change the past! Because this is obviously doomed to fail, it is understandable why such preoccupation leads to drinking, drug using, bingeing, and other destructive behaviors that are pathological responses to distress, in this case the distress of frustration when one is trying to accomplish the impossible.

Some people have difficulty with forgiveness. They cannot forgive others and they cannot forgive themselves, and usually both go together. Simple, rational thinking will pose the question, "What is it that you want me to do about my misbehavior of the past? It is understandable that I should try to compensate wherever possible, but beyond that, what else can I do? Will anyone benefit by my wearing sackcloth and flagellating myself?

Clearly one cannot dismiss mistakes with a superficial apology. Simply saying "I'm sorry" is not a magic incantation that can eradicate wrongs that were done. However, when a misdeed is sincerely regretted and a dedicated commitment not to repeat the misdeed has been made, refusal to forgive is cruel. This is as true of refusal to forgive oneself as it is of refusal to forgive another.

Harboring resentments drains one's energies. One recovering alcoholic expressed this quaintly. "Harboring resentments is letting someone you don't like live inside your head rent-free." Because two things cannot occupy the same space at the same time, the mind that is occupied with resentments cannot accommodate constructive thinking. Again, this is equally valid when the resentments are against oneself.

Spirituality is a positive process, and there is no room for negative attitudes in spirituality.

CHAPTER 26

Joy

Let a joy keep you. Reach out your hands and take it
when it runs by.

CARL SANDBURG

Spirituality is joy.

Joy can be experienced at various levels. If you give a small
child a shiny, colorful little object, his eyes may sparkle and he
may squeal with glee at this new possession. This same object
given to a mature adult would hardly elicit such a reaction.
Indeed, if an adult were to react similarly over a relatively
worthless object, we would be correct in assuming that the
poor person has never progressed beyond an infantile mental
development. The joy of spirituality is one that should befit us
as mature, thinking people.

We have stressed the importance of having a purpose in life as
one of the essential ingredients of spirituality. Lack of purpose
significantly detracts from joy. Consider the story of the man
who was sentenced to twenty-five years imprisonment at hard
labor, whose work assignment consisted of being shackled to

the handle of an immense wheel that was fixed in a wall, and all day he was to turn this massive wheel.

The man would often reflect upon what it was that he was achieving with this never-ending exertion. Perhaps he was grinding wheat into flour, or perhaps he was generating energy that was somehow being constructively utilized.

After completion of the twenty-five-year sentence, the shackles were removed, and the man, exhausted and aching with pain, was freed. His first act was to go to the other side of the wall. Imagine his shock and dismay when he discovered that on the other side of the wall there was nothing! The wheel was not connected to anything. All these years he had exerted his energy for no purpose at all. Neither man nor beast had benefitted from his hard labor. Broken in spirit as well as in body, the man wept bitterly. The awareness that all his back-breaking work for so many years had been for naught was worse than the suffering of the hard labor.

We may escape thinking about what it is that we are to achieve with our lives, but such escape is not always possible. If we ever have moments of reckoning, the lack of a purpose in life will haunt us.

Have you ever wondered why it is that the beginning of a new year is so widely celebrated with revelry and intoxication?

Reflect for a moment. Everyone is shouting "Happy New Year." If they are really all that happy about this great moment, why would they want to be intoxicated and therefore unaware of that sensation of happiness? After all, alcohol is technically an emotional anesthetic, and it is absurd to kill a pleasant feeling of accomplishment. If one were truly happy, he would wish to savor happiness and preserve it rather than abolish it with a chemical.

The reason for this behavior on New Year's Eve is that the introduction of a new year also marks the closure of the past year, and the passage of a very significant unit of time in one's life. If one were to reflect on the past year and were to realize how it had been foolishly squandered, and that one had not grown appreciably, if at all during that time, and that a true reckoning would show the past year to be essentially wasted, that would be depressing indeed. No wonder people anesthetize themselves when in a state of disappointment and disillusion.

The purpose, therefore, of drinking to intoxication on New Year's Eve is to avoid reflection upon failure and to banish the awareness of the relative futility of the past year. But people who can look back upon the past year with a realization that it has been meaningful and that it has been one of growth and achievement do not need to drink themselves into oblivion to greet the onset of a new year.

The first of January is not the only time when we are prone to make a reckoning. Our thinking brain can confront us many times and question the meaning of our existence. The spiritual person who sees his life as having been purposeful and who can look forward to continuing to live purposefully can experience joy. The person devoid of spirituality can only try to deflect this question of his meaning or lack thereof by various kinds of distraction or by using chemicals to suppress the brain and prevent it from generating stress.

When the purpose in life is fulfilling the Divine wish, yet another dimension of joy is added.

How proud a person would be if he were given an audience with a head of state! How privileged a person would feel if the president of the United States or the queen of England appointed him to a special committee or commissioned him as an ambassador! Yet these prominent people are human, mere mortals like ourselves, and their dominion is but temporal. How honored and privileged a person should feel to know that in prayer he has an audience with the Sovereign of the universe, who has commissioned him to fulfill a particular function,.

Growth in spirituality should be elating. If one watches an infant beginning to crawl or take his first steps, one can see the jubilation and excitement as the child masters ambulation. One can see the infant's probing curiosity and the thrill that accompanies each new discovery he makes. That is how we can feel when growing spiritually. Each character development raises one to a new level, and each new insight into the wonders of the universe brings us to a greater realization of the majesty of God. Thus in spiritual growth, joy can be born from frustration and be nourished by effort and challenge.

A noted theologian was approached by a student, who complained of his frustration in trying to come closer to God. "I do not understand it. There have been times when I have felt myself just within the reach of God, then abruptly I feel myself more distant than ever."

"That is quite as it should be," the master said. "Consider the scene where a father is teaching his infant child how to walk. He waits until the child has developed sufficiently to stand upright. Then he places himself immediately in front of the child, and extends his hands, beckoning the child to come to him. The child, seeing the father's hands only inches away, feels secure enough to venture taking the first step. Once the child has taken the first step, the father retreats a bit further, and again beckons to the child. Having safely taken the first step and seeing the father still close, the child is willing to risk taking another step. Again the father retreats, and continues to do so, each time distancing himself further and further away, and encouraging the child to come to him."

"If we were to enter the mind of the child, we would find that the child is bewildered. 'What is going on here?' he wondered. 'I am trying to reach my father, and the more effort I make, the further away he gets.'"

"What is happening is that the goals of the father and that of the child are disparate. The child's goal is to reach the father, but that is not the father's goal at all. The father could easily reach down and lift the child to him at any time, and would indeed take great pleasure in doing so. But the father wishes to teach the child how to walk independently, and this development of the child's ability requires the stratagem of progressively distancing himself from the child."

"And so it is," continued the master, "with you and your desire to reach God. Your intent is indeed commendable, but just as with the child, the moment you reach your goal, your growth and development would come to an end. God wishes to increase your spiritual capabilities, and this necessitates Him distancing Himself from you just when you happen to be close to Him."

Learning to walk may be frustrating to a young child, but to a mature person who understands that his frustration is actually an indication of spiritual growth, even the frustration itself can be a source of joy.

There is hardly a person who has been spared misery of one kind or another in life. Pain and suffering generate anger, resentment, and depression, which often linger beyond the incident precipitating the distress. These feelings may cast their gloom over a person's life, so that he is unable to enjoy those things in life which could provide him with happiness.

The spiritual person who has developed a trust in Divine judgment may not be able to rejoice at the moment he experiences distress, but when distress has passed, his trust in God and the belief that what transpired is somehow for his ultimate good allows him to free himself of the bitterness of the anger and resentment, and to enjoy the good things that life has to offer.

The pleasures one can derive from gratifying physical drives are very ephemeral. A person may indeed enjoy a gourmet dinner, but one day afterward, it is but a memory. However, the knowledge that one has been of help to another person, and that at this very moment another person may be living a better life because of help that was extended twenty years earlier, continues to provide a pleasant feeling of long duration. In this way, spiritual behavior adds to enduring happiness. When parents give their children gifts, and the children use these wisely, it is a source of pleasure to the parents. If children squander their parental gifts, or use them in a destructive manner, it is a source of grief to the parents. When we use our abilities wisely and partake of worldly goods judiciously, we may assume that this pleases God. As a child rejoices with the knowledge that his parents are pleased so, too, do we rejoice when we feel we are pleasing God.

The world is ours to enjoy, but to enjoy wisely. When we live a spiritual life, avoid indulgence, and partake of the Divine blessings as befits a spiritual person, we may be certain that the divine Father is pleased with us, and this should afford us no small measure of joy.

In twelve-step programs, we hear much about gratitude, particularly gratitude for being sober, and for having been given another chance.

Gratitude and joy are closely intertwined. Just as harboring resentments detracts from joy, so does gratitude enhance joy. This was clearly the intent of the psalmist who wrote, "A Psalm of Gratitude." *Serve God with joy, come before Him with song* (100, 1–2).

Many people are so alienated from spontaneous feelings of joy that they can laugh only if their funny bone is tickled by a professional comedian. Bombarded by superfluous worries, they are anxious during the day and unable to sleep at night. Their facial expression betrays their state of tension and apprehensiveness. Let me illustrate with a rather extreme case, a true caricature, which sheds light on an acute case of apprehension in which joy was shackled by fear.

A fifty-two-year-old woman was referred to me by another psychiatrist because of anxiety and insomnia. He had been unsuccessful in relieving her symptoms.

The woman was a widow, whose wealthy husband had died several years earlier, and who had left her a very sizeable estate. Her money was well invested and she had a substantial income. Her problem was that because no *new* money was being generated as was the case when her husband was alive, she was worried that her fortune might become so depleted by inflation that when she was ready for a nursing home, there would not be enough money for a high-quality facility.

Now this same woman came to her sessions bedecked with diamonds. One time she complained that the mansion she lived in was too difficult to maintain, and when I suggested that she move to a smaller house, she responded that the task of moving all her belongings was too formidable. "Why, I have over fifty thousand dollars worth of linens alone." This woman could have used her money to travel around the world and enjoy so much of the beauty and the wonders of the world. She could have lived for a thousand years without depleting her assets, yet she could not find any peace and suffered the torments of pointless worry. She was not able to be grateful for what she had, and because she was plagued by the fear of being impoverished, had no joy at all.

I could not help this woman any more than the three psychiatrists that had preceded me. Unfortunately, she had never turned to alcohol or drugs. Had she been addicted and hit bottom, she may have found a source of help in a twelve-step fellowship. There she would learn to live one day at a time and not take on problems that are beyond her control, such as her unwarranted fear of spending her old age in an inadequate nursing home.

Most people's worries may be more realistic than this woman's, but indulging in worry about problems over which we have no control is pointless. Being bound by worry prevents us from being grateful for whatever we do have, and will inhibit joy and our pleasure in life.

Purposefulness, trust, avoiding indulgence and excess, gratitude, and living one day at a time are not only noble attributes of character, but are aspects of a lifestyle that permits the attainment of joy.

CHAPTER 27

Worship Whom?

Trust in God with your whole heart, and do not lean on
your own understanding.

PROVERBS 3:5

In order to make a reasonable decision, a person must be aware
of what his options are. Not knowing what options are available may cause a person to make a foolish decision.

A father confronted his daughter's boyfriend, "What are
your intentions, young man, honorable or dishonorable?"

The young man responded, "You mean I get a choice?"

We sometimes think we have options that really do not
exist.

Let me place a proposition before you: Man is a creature of
worship.

There is much evidence that since time immemorial and in
places vastly separated from one another, man has always
worshipped something. Primitive man worshipped the sun,
moon, and various objects or forces of nature. Later, some
systemization of religion appeared in paganism, and finally,

civilized man arrived at monotheism. However, worship was always around.

If, indeed, it is inherent within man that he worship, then the option is not whether he will or will not worship, but whether he will worship himself or something external to himself. Worship is here defined as adoration, prayer, and trust, individually or in combination.

When worship is of something external, it may be worship of God, or the state, or some ideal to which the person dedicates himself. If worship is not of something external, the only remaining option is worship of oneself, which takes the form of egocentricity.

I alluded to this a bit earlier, when I pointed out that people who claim that they are atheists and hence cannot participate in a twelve-step program because it is God-oriented are deluding themselves. They *do* believe in a God, but consider themselves to be their own God.

There is such a thing as a healthy ego. I am a very important part of my world. However, it is essential that I know my proper place in the world, what I can expect of myself, and what I can expect of the world. When the "I" is disproportionately great, egocentricity or egomania exists.

In egocentricity, the ego becomes a tyrant whose demands are insatiable. Everything an egotist does is in service of the ego, because he essentially worships himself. An irony of egocentricity is that the person is apt to vehemently deny that he is the center of his own world. He is quick to point out that *other people* are egocentric, but certainly not he. Often this is just a projection of his own egocentricity on others. By projecting thusly the egotist deludes himself that he is not egocentric.

Egocentricity breeds misery, because the demands of the egocentric person are rarely met. The inflated ego of the egocentric requires that others appreciate him and that they manifest this appreciation by showing him what he considers appropriate respect. If he is not greeted in the manner he feels is his due, if he is not given honorable mention, or if he is not seated in a place of distinction, he is deeply irritated. He may manifest this displeasure, or he may suppress it. In either case, his attitude conveys itself, and does not buy him any friendship. His extreme sensitivity may actually alienate people, and when he finds himself rejected rather than welcome, he is deeply hurt, and becomes even more demanding.

The egocentric person deludes himself because he fears the truth, which is in fact something that merits no fear at all. The truth is that the person would be well-liked if he had a realistic self-awareness. His hurt feelings are fed by delusion, as is his inflated sense of importance. The egocentric knows no happiness as long as he remains a victim of his delusions. Trying to satisfy an egocentric is like trying to fill a bottomless pit.

The difference between healthy and unhealthy emotions is often quantitative. It is only natural that a person wishes to be appreciated by others, and a person who is not subject to inordinate needs for recognition can enjoy being appreciated. However, if one constantly dreams of achieving fame, glory, riches, or great achievements not only in order to be admired, but also to feel vindicated, one is probably egocentric. A person may protest that his desire to make an epochal discovery is only in order to benefit mankind. If that was completely true, then one should be just as happy if that discovery was made by someone else. One can be both altruistic and also enjoy being recognized. Someone who professes to be purely altruistic and to have no need for appreciation is probably defensive and denying his craving for recognition.

I once interviewed a very successful businessman who was hospitalized for peptic ulcer disease. He had been active in many civic projects, but was unable to enjoy the abundant recognition he had achieved. "One wall of my living room is covered with testimonial plaques," he said, "but they mean nothing to me." The egocentric is unable to enjoy doing for others and is discontent even with his own achievements.

Another characteristic of an egocentric person is that he is likely to vehemently deny any form of dependency in himself. Egocentrics in dire physical straits have been known to walk out of hospitals because they cannot accept legitimate help. Accepting help is demeaning to them, and is intolerable to the fragile, inflated ego. Those familiar with the alcoholic, whose life is disintegrating but who continues to protest that he can set everything straight without help from any one, are witness to a classic example of how threatening the acceptance of help can be to the egocentric.

It is the nature of the human being to be dependent, and this should not be in the least demeaning. When dependency is so exaggerated that one refrains from doing for himself whatever he can, and depends on others to do everything for him, then this dependency is pathologic. When one does for himself everything that is feasible, his dependency on others, whether on another person or on God, is a healthy dependency.

When Gateway Rehabilitation Center was in its planning phase, I met with psychoanalysts who had been my instructors in psychiatry. When they heard that I was going to fashion the Center to be compatible with twelve-step programs, they were critical. "All you will be doing is taking the person's dependency off of the bottle and transferring it onto AA," they said. I asked them to tell me in absolute honesty whether they had ever succeeded, even with years of psychoanalytic treatment, in making a dependent person nondependent. Gradually they had to admit that even with their greatest therapeutic triumphs, a sick dependency was invariably converted into a healthy dependency.

The spiritual person is free of obnoxious egocentricity. He worships God rather than himself, and knows the goal of his existence is to fulfill some purpose other than gratifying his own desires. His demands are therefore not excessive, and he is not a victim of the chronic fear of one whose desires can never be satisfied. He accepts dependence upon God as natural, and not in the least demeaning. By the same token, he is not deflated by the realization that he may be dependent upon other people for things that are beyond his capacities. He is not overly dependent, because he has a sense of duty and responsibility. He can like himself and be liked by others, because he neither clings to people nor repels them.

Spirituality enables a person to be at peace with God, with other people, and with himself.

CHAPTER 28

Spirituality in the Psalms

*This is the prayer of a poor person at a time of anguish,
when he pours his words before God.*
PSALMS 102:1

A rich source of spirituality in literature is found in the Book of Psalms. In contrast to the other scriptures, such as the prophets, which are essentially God speaking to man, the psalms are the expressions and outpouring of man's heart to God. In the psalms we find expression of emotion: anguish, joy, and hope in the face of desperation. We find adoration of God and an appreciation of the beauty of the universe. Let us sample just a few excerpts.

> *Favor me once again, O God, and in the abundance of
>   Your compassion, erase my sins...*
> *For I know my sins, and my iniquities are ever before
>   me...*
> *Create for me a pure heart, and renew a steadfast spirit
>   within me...*

Restore to me the joy of Your salvation, and let the spirit of
*   free devotion uphold me,*
Then I will teach the sinful Your ways, and the errant will
*   return to you . . .*

                                                    (51:3-15)

In these verses the psalmist is keenly aware of his mistakes,
and indeed, feels it necessary to remember them so that he does
not repeat them, but he does not ruminate and brood over
them. To the contrary, once he has resolved not to repeat his
misdeeds, he is confident that not only will God erase his sins,
but will also provide him with joy and happiness. Relieved of
the burden of his sins, and confident that God will grant him
joy, he now resolves to become a new person, and prays to God
to allow him a new start and endow him with a fresh spirit. A
new and hopeful personality now emerges, ready and able to
live life to its fullest, and offering help to his fellow man.

Be gracious to me, O God, for I am crushed, heal me for
*   my bones are afflicted.*
And my soul is stricken; O God, how long will You allow
*   this to continue?*
Return, O God, and free my soul, help me by virtue of
*   Your mercy . . .*
I am weary with sighing, I melt away my bed with tears . . .
But God has heard my pleas, and He accepts my prayer . . .

                                                    (6:3-10)

We hear the cries of anguish, the profuse weeping, and the
exhaustion of suffering. "How long, O God, will I need to
suffer so?" Then we hear the tranquility, that even while in
pain, there is the comfort that God has heard one's prayer.

There is the unparalleled grandeur of Psalm 104, beautiful in
any translation, but so majestic in the original that it has been

said that it is worthwhile to learn Hebrew if only to read this psalm in the original.

> *Praise God, O my soul,*
> *My God, You are so great, garbed in glory and Magnificence,*
> *Who dons light as a garment, and unfurls the heavens as a carpet...*
> *He makes the winds His messengers, and flaming fires His ministers...*
> *He sends forth springs into brooks, that they may run between mountains,*
> *To give drink to the beasts of the field, and the creatures of the forest quench their thirst.*
> *Thereby dwell the birds of the heavens, who lift up their voices from among the clefts...*
> *The trees of God also have their fill, the cedars of Lebanon which He has planted,*
> *Where the birds make their nests, the stork making its home in the cypress trees.*
> *The high mountains are for the wild goats, and the rocks are a refuge for the hares...*
> *The young lions roar after their prey, and also seek their food from God.*
> *When the sun rises they gather and crouch in their dens...*
> *How great and manifold are Your works, O God, with wisdom You have made them all, the earth is full of Your possessions...*
>
> *(104:1-24)*

These verses need no comment. They allow one's spirit to soar as one sees the majesty of God everywhere in nature.

Then there is a psalm that appeals to anyone who has experienced suffering, but which recovering alcoholics or addicts may well believe was written exclusively for them.

When the pains of death oppressed me, when the straits of
Hell gained over me, when I faced anguish and sorrow;
Then I called upon the name of God, "I beg of You, O
God, rescue my soul."
God is ready to grant grace and is just, and our God is
merciful.
God watches over those who are unaware, and when I was
brought low He granted me new life.
Return to peace, my soul, for God is kind to you...

(116:3-7)

How well we know that God watches over the simple, protecting them when they act in folly. Ask any recovered addict and he will tell you of countless times when God intervened to save him from death, and of the peace and tranquility that comes when one accepts Divine benevolence.

What does it mean to be spiritual? Listen to the psalmist.

O God, who shall sojourn in Your tabernacle?
Who shall dwell upon the mountain of Your sanctuary?
He that walks in moral integrity, practices righteousness,
and speaks the truth in his heart.
He who bears no slander on his tongue, nor does evil to his
fellow, nor casts aspersion upon his neighbor.
In whose eyes that which is blameworthy is despised, and
who honors those who revere God

(15:1-4)

One must trust in God even when one feels abandoned by Him, even when one feels one's prayers have not been heard.

My God, my God, why have You forsaken me?...
My God, I call out by day, and You do not answer, and at
night there is no pacification for me...
Our forefathers trusted in You and You saved them...

They trusted in You and they were not deceived...
For You are He who wrested me from the womb, who gave
*   me trust upon my mother's breast.*
It is upon You that I have been cast from my birth, You are
*   my God from my mother's womb.*

                                        (22:2-11)

The craving to be close to God.
As a deer pants for the springs of water,
So my soul thirsts after You, O God.
My soul thirsts for God, for the living God,
When shall I come again and see myself before the face of
*   God?*

                                        (42:2-3)

The folly of making attainment of material wealth one's goal
    in life:

Hear this, all you nations. Give ear all you inhabitants of
*   the fleeting world.*
Sons of man and sons of men alike, rich and poor together...
As for those that put their trust in their wealth and who
*   glory in the multitude of their riches,*
Yet not one of them can redeem his brother with it, nor
*   give it to God as ransom.*
For them the redemption of their own soul is too costly...
Yet he desires to live on forever, and thinks he will never
*   see the grave...*
They think their houses are forever, their dwelling places
*   from generation to generation, because they have*
*   proclaimed their names throughout the lands...*
This is their way, their folly remains with them...
But God will redeem my soul from the power of the grave,
*   by taking me to Himself.*

> *Therefore do not be afraid when one waxes rich, when the*
> *splendor of his house is great,*
> *For when he dies, he shall carry nothing with him, his*
> *splendor shall not follow him.*

(49:2-18)

We could continue to cite many excerpts, but these few should suffice to direct one to this wonderful and abundant reservoir of spirituality.

CHAPTER 29

Carrying the Message

What is the right course that a person should choose?
One which does credit to him who adopts it, and also
earns him the respect of others.

<small>ETHICS OF THE FATHERS 2:1</small>

Step Twelve: *Having had a spiritual awakening as a result of
these steps, we tried to carry this message to alcoholics, and to
practice these principles in all our affairs.*

Although this step does not appear to be directly concerned
with spirituality per se, but with "carrying the message," it
does nevertheless contain something relevant to spirituality,
when combined with one of the Traditions. According to the
Twelfth Tradition, the fellowship's public relations are based on
attraction rather than promotion. Anyone who desires what the
fellowship has to offer is welcome. If someone wishes to have
program literature, it is available to him. No one hands out
literature on street corners, or canvasses door-to-door, or con-
ducts mail promotions. No one proselytizes. People who belong
to twelve-step fellowships do not go to bars, drug hangouts,

casinos, or ice cream parlors to make converts for abstinence from alcohol, drugs, gambling, or overeating.

Why is this important to spirituality? Because if a person is comfortable and secure with his own convictions, he has no need to make others "see the truth." Perhaps it is too broad a generalization, but when people try to convert others to their way of thinking it is often for an ulterior motive: the need to reinforce one's own fragile conviction.

There are some obstinate stalwarts who still insist that the earth is flat, and that all arguments to the contrary can be disproved. Pictures taken from satellites that show the earth to be spherical are dismissed as sheer trickery. Although this seems ludicrous to me, I do not have the slightest inclination to convince these people that they are mistaken. I know for certain that the earth is spherical, and it does not bother me in the least that some people think otherwise. However, if I were shaky in my convictions, and it were important for me to believe a certain way, I would feel threatened if people disagreed, and especially if they had cogent arguments to rebut my belief.

Most people who come to a twelve-step program have invariably tried a number of other ways to curb their addiction, and have discovered that half-measures are of no avail, and that only a program that emphasizes and incorporates spirituality is effective.

People who recover through these programs are sufficiently firm in their own convictions that they have no need to make others believe as they do. If you come for help and wish to know what has worked for them, they will be more than happy to share their hope, strength, and courage, but they will not run after you.

Another feature of true spirituality is that it does not come with a price tag. Like the air we breathe, spirituality is free. If someone charges for spirituality, there is reason to suspect that there is a motive for personal gain rather than a search for truth. An outstanding feature of the twelve-step fellowships is that no one stands to gain monetarily, and there is no membership fee. If one wishes to donate something to cover rental of the meeting rooms and the cost of coffee and doughnuts, he is free to do so. If one does not wish to contribute, no one will criticize him. And if a person happens to be in such dire straits that he takes a dollar *out* of the basket as it is being passed, people will understand.

In addition to lack of monetary gain, spirituality does not require a charismatic leader who demands adoration. The twelve-step programs do not have leaders in the sense of superiors who make authoritative decisions and exert control over other people's lives. Each group is independent and operates according to the dictates of the group conscience, guided only by the Twelve Traditions. This prevents the possibility of abuse by persons craving power who might seek to influence the group by appealing to personal interests or outside causes in any way.

In the midst of the twentieth century, society was racked by a cultural upheaval epitomized by the slogan "God is dead." The unprecedented scientific breakthroughs led man to believe that he was omnipotent and that he could control everything in the world. But, in fact, there was little control and society verged on total disarray. Throughout the disillusionment with science and within a context of social upheaval a panicky search for spirituality developed. Some misguided individuals sought spirituality in mind-expansion through hallucinogenic drugs. Others flocked to causes that promised escape from a meaningless existence. Still others in their desperation failed to see that they were being exploited by "spiritual" leaders who were preaching spirituality while amassing great material fortunes.

The twelve-step fellowships offer a program for spiritual

development. The terms are broad enough so that one is not required to accept any particular idea of God, there is no militia to bring in non-believers, and there is no one person or group who will stand to gain in any special way from the fellowships. The fellowships have demonstrated that striving for character improvement can be attractive. People are indeed motivated by the pursuit of happiness, and when they see anything that holds a promise of happiness, they will be drawn to it. There are people who, on their first encounter with an AA meeting, remark, "I must be in the wrong place. If everyone here is abstinent from alcohol, how can they all smile, laugh, and seem to be happy?"

It is this kind of "carrying the message" that is characteristic of true spirituality. Life becomes meaningful, purposeful, and goal-directed. People begin to see themselves not as *homo sapiens*, but as *homo spiritus*, and while no one claims perfection, everyone strives in his own way to become the ideal human being, a being created in the image of "God as I understand Him."

AFTERWORD

The summation of it: after all has been heard, revere
God and observe His commandments, for that is the
essence of man.

E C C L E S I A S T E S   1 2 : 1 2

It should be evident that virtually everything that spirituality
offers the recovering addict can be of equal advantage to the
nonaddict and indeed to mankind as a whole. The trait of
going for short-term gain or immediate gratification at the
expense of the long-term loss is certainly not unique to addicts.
Nor is rationalizing such foolish behavior unique to chemically
dependent people. Our society as a whole is mottled with this
destructive pattern.

What can we say about a culture that systematically poisons
the air we breathe, pollutes the water we drink, contaminates
the soil with radioactive and other toxic materials that find their
way into the food we eat, and sprays cancer-causing pesticides
on the fruits and vegetables we consume? All of the industries
that stand to profit from the results of these destructive acts
have abundant rationalizations whose purpose is to demon-

strate that all this is somehow beneficial to mankind. We raze our forests, strip-mine our soil, exterminate many species of animals, and fill the skies with chemicals that threaten to convert our world into an uninhabitable hothouse, and all this is so that man should have a "better" life. Highly educated people inhale smoke that causes cancer and emphysema, and the same government that officially condemns cigarettes as a leading cause of death and disability gives bountiful subsidies to the tobacco growers that produce the poison, while the tobacco industry spends hundreds of millions of dollars to assist smokers in their denial and rationalization. Last but not least, the media lure young people to consume alcohol with titillating advertisements that imply that drinking will make them more masculine or more sensuous.

Strangely enough, governmental departments are willing to spend huge sums of money to prevent alcoholism and drug addiction. Legislators and bureaucrats are constantly searching for laws and regulations that will reduce addiction. With cultural habits, policies, and practices that are so pro-addiction in their character being overtly and covertly condoned and promoted, how does any sensible person expect efforts to discourage people from seizing the momentary gratification and ignoring the long-term loss to be the least bit effective?

The alcoholic or drug addict does not abandon his behavior until he hits a "rock bottom," at which time the aggregate of the noxious consequences of addiction finally make him realize how destructive it is to seek immediate gratification at the risk of ultimate disaster. There are alcoholics who are brought to their senses by a crisis but many unfortunately continue to their ultimate self-destruction.

What course will our civilization take? Will it seize upon the principles of spirituality and pull itself out of a nosedive, or will it continue a relentless course of seeking immediate gratification, supported by denial and rationalization, until it is too late?

In the final analysis, spirituality is a quality of relationships: man to man, and man to God. However, this is not a case of either/or. It is much closer to all or none. Unless one relates properly to both, one is not relating properly to either.

History as well as contemporary events have documented what happens when people preoccupy themselves only with God, and are not spiritual in relation to their fellow man. Religion then deteriorates into religiosity, often an affected, self-serving piety and that can lead to the cruelest of atrocities committed in the name of God. Love of God that is devoid of love of one's fellow man often proves to be an egocentric self-love, the very antithesis of spirituality.

God is not comprised of component parts. To reject part of God is to reject all of God. If we believe that the spirit of God is within each human being, the rejection of any one person is tantamount to rejecting God. Spirituality is thus the wholeness of man's relationship to his world, a wholeness that can make him whole.